THE MAN IN CELL NO. 1

THE MAN IN CELL NO. 1

Dedicated to the old fashioned
prayer meeting

By Lee Roberson

SWORD of the LORD
PUBLISHERS
P.O. BOX 1099, MURFREESBORO, TN 37133

Printed and Bound in the United States of America

*The sermons of this book were preached
in the midweek prayer services of the
Highland Park Baptist Church,
Chattanooga, Tennessee*

Table of Contents

Preface

"THREE TO THRIVE"
"THE SWEETEST SERVICE OF THE WEEK"

An essential for a growing, happy, powerful church is a great midweek service!

I began my ministry at Highland Park Baptist Church in 1942 on a Wednesday evening. I established at once in the hearts of our people the importance of three vital services per week—Sunday morning, Sunday evening, and Wednesday evening. The "Three to Thrive" motto soon came into being. We continued with this emphasis for forty years and six months. I concluded my ministry at Highland Park on Wednesday evening, April 27, 1983.

There is power in prayer! The midweek service is a time of prayer. I believe its chief importance is to emphasize the power of prayer, and to encourage God's people to spend much time in private prayer and in the family altar.

"The Sweetest Service of the Week" was a time of singing, praying and preaching. An invitation was given at the close of each service, and for forty years and six months there was a response to every invitation. People were saved in the prayer meetings, and hundreds followed Christ in believer's baptism.

In every service the full choir sang and the orchestra played, and special music was given.

In the midst of every service there was a time of prayer. The prayer list was read and then three or four men from the audience were called to the platform to lead in prayer.

The service for more than forty years followed this general outline:

A vigorous, happy song service—three or four songs carefully chosen by Dr. J. R. Faulkner.

A special song—solos, duets, trios, quartets and the choir were heard.

A season of prayer—a lengthy prayer list was read, telling of people who were ill at home or in the hospitals. This list also included the bereaved. This mimeographed list was given to each person in the audience. At the prayer time, men were called from the congregation to lead in prayer.

Next, announcements and the offering—announcements were given for all divisions of our work. After the announcements, we received an offering for missions. Every penny of the prayer service offering was placed in the missionary fund. (I need to say that all Sunday evening offerings were also designated for missions. In addition to this, over fifty percent of the regular church offerings were used to support missionaries in all parts of the world. In my fortieth year as pastor, we were giving assistance to 565 missionaries in various parts of the world.)

After the offering, a message from the Word of God—the message was prayerfully given to encourage Christians and to lay upon their hearts a burden for a lost and dying world.

After the sermon, the invitation: urging the lost to accept Christ, inviting Christians to unite with our church, and calling Christians to give themselves fully to Christ and to His service. There were blessed results week after week.

Through the years many testified that the prayer service was truly "the sweetest service of the week." Hence, we constantly emphasized to every member—"Be a prayer meeting Christian."

Dr. Lee Roberson
Pastor Emeritus, Highland Park Baptist Church
Founder/Chancellor, Tennessee Temple Schools

The Man in Cell #1

"And they had then a notable prisoner, called Barabbas."— Matt. 27:16.

Christ died for sinners!

This pungent fact is given again and again in the Scriptures.

It was given by the prophets.

It was given by the Psalmist David.

It was given by the angel announcing the birth of Christ.

It was given by the Lord Himself.

It was given by the writers of the epistles.

But a further illustration of this truth is given in the story before us.

Jesus was standing before Pilate. Pilate desired to release the Lord. Without question, he saw the innocency of the Saviour.

Then the governor had a brilliant idea: Give them a choice—a choice between Jesus and a notable prisoner called Barabbas. It seems likely that Pilate thought he had settled the matter. Surely the people would demand the release of Jesus and let Barabbas die.

Ah, but when the matter was laid before them, they cried out for the release of Barabbas and for the crucifixion of Jesus Christ.

Barabbas was freed, and Christ went to the cross and died. He died in the place of Barabbas, but Christ died in the stead of all sinners.

"For when we were yet without strength, in due time Christ died for the ungodly."—Rom. 5:6.

"But God commendeth his love toward us, in that, while we were yet sinners, Christ died for us."—Rom. 5:8.

"Who his own self bare our sins in his own body on the tree. . . . "—I Pet. 2:24.

Now let us think about this man in cell number one. He was

I. DISTINGUISHED BY SIN

"And they had then a notable prisoner, called Barabbas."— Matt. 27:16.

"And there was one named Barabbas, which lay bound with them that had made insurrection with him, who had committed murder in the insurrection."—Mark 15:7.

"And they cried out all at once, saying, Away with this man, and release unto us Barabbas: (Who for a certain sedition made in the city, and for murder, was cast into prison.)"—Luke 23:18,19.

"Then cried they all again, saying, Not this man, but Barabbas. Now Barabbas was a robber."—John 18:40.

It seems a sad commentary on a life when nothing good can be said for a man. I have known a few of this kind—search and search, yet no good thing could be said. The family could not find a good word nor could the neighbors.

Distinguished by sin! The world has had many of this kind. Those who are distinguished by the sins of drunkenness, sins of immorality, sins of dishonesty, sins of infidelity.

Ordinarily, something good can be found by someone. But as far as we can tell, the man in cell number one was distinguished only by his sin.

The man in cell number one was

II. LOST

The Bible tells us that he was a "notable" sinner. He was condemned by the law to die.

But more than this: as far as we know, this man was eternally lost. He was a sinner, "without God and without hope in the world."

Lost—but not because of his wicked life.

Lost—but not because of his jail sentence.

Lost—because he had not accepted Christ as Saviour.

Lost—because of his unbelief.

John 3:18 has a message that should be heeded by everyone: "He that believeth on him is not condemned: but he that believeth not is condemned already, because he hath not believed in the name of the only begotten Son of God."

This Bible plainly tells us that a man is condemned by one single sin—the sin of unbelief. Barabbas was only a few feet away from the Christ and yet lost. You may be but inches or seconds away from Christ; and yet without Him, you are lost.

Salvation is without question the greatest thing in the entire world. Yet how often people turn away from it and tie onto some insignificant, unimportant, unworthy thing.

One of the soldiers of Alexander the Great, while searching for treasures in the palace of Darius, found a leather bag containing the almost priceless crown jewels of Persia. They were worth millions, but the stupid soldier was ignorant to the value of jewels. In fact, he did not know a jewel when he saw one. So he shook out the little glittering stones into the rubbish heap, saved the leather bag and went on boasting about the fine bag he had found for carrying his food.

The story speaks for itself. Many of you would say, "What a foolish man!" Yet how many turn away from salvation—the gift of God—and go on holding to their paltry effects.

The man in cell number one was

III. UNLOVED BY MAN

We cannot be positive about this; yet as far as we know, the world cared nothing for Barabbas, the outcast. He had sinned against society. He was caught, imprisoned and sentenced to die.

The world has little affection for its own. A man may think he has many friends; but, in fact, the world cares nothing for others. The world is selfish. It drops its own when the value of a person is gone.

My memory takes me back to the story of a man whom I tried

to win to the Saviour. He lived in our city. When I went to see him, he boasted of his many friends. He told of his success in the business world; then in answer to my arguments regarding his need of Christ, he stated, "I have need of no one. I have money. I have friends. I do not need the One you are talking about."

You will remember in my recitation of this account in days gone by: A few days after I had paid my visit to the man, he died. I went to his funeral. Beside the preacher and me, there were exactly five people present. The man who had boasted of his many friends died friendless.

But let me hasten to say this: Though unloved by man, the sinner is still loved by God. Once again, let your mind think upon Romans 5:8: "But God commendeth his love toward us, in that, while we were yet sinners, Christ died for us."

How can we escape the beauty of the most familiar verse in the Bible, John 3:16: "For God so loved the world, that he gave his only begotten Son, that whosoever believeth in him should not perish, but have everlasting life"?

John tells us, "Herein is love, not that we loved God, but that he loved us, and sent his Son to be the propitiation for our sins" (I John 4:10).

The man in cell number one

IV. HAD HEARD THE CHIEF PHILOSOPHY OF MEN

Yes, you have heard it, too.

What is it? "Live right," "Do the best you can," "Be sincere." Yes, the man in cell number one had heard it and had failed to live up to it. His eyes had been fastened on the lowly, sinful things of earth. He had no time for higher things.

Take warning from this story. Man needs to look up: fastening the eyes upon lowly things can only bring danger and loss.

Dr. Charles M. Tibbetts told about an experience of his childhood:

> When I was a small boy, a chimney was built on the outside of the church which stood near my home. With a boy's curiosity, I watched the men proceed with the work. How I longed to climb the ladder and stand on the staging as it rose up above

the very top of the lofty roof! But my mother had warned me that I was not to interfere with the workmen; and of all things, I was not to climb ladders. So I had to content myself with watching from my humble place on the ground.

Then one day one of the men leaned out of the edge of the staging and shouted down to me, "Boy, there's a trowel there on the ground. Bring it up here." That was the most thrilling moment of my young life! I grasped the trowel firmly and climbed with it to the height where the men were working.

As I approached the staging, I heard the other man say to the one who had told me to come up, "You ought not to have got him up here. When he looks down, he will be so scared he may fall."

For the moment my attention was placed upon the importance of my errand—the delivery of the trowel. But when that was done, true to the perversity of our nature, I looked down to see for myself what it was that would frighten me so greatly as to make me liable to fall.

Being a mere child, the distance was appalling. I felt sick and dizzy. Overwhelmed, I would have fallen had I not at that instant heard the assuring voice of my friend say, *"Look up, lad. Keep looking up!"*

Strength and control returned to my muscles and nerves. As I descended, I kept my eyes turned upward to the men on the staging. All the while as he laid his bricks, one of them kept saying, "Look up, lad. Keep looking up!"

An important lesson for every one of us—keep looking up! When we look down, life fails and we falter and fall. When we look up, we receive new courage and inspiration from our God.

The world cannot save a man! Salvation is by looking unto the Son of God.

> I've a message from the Lord, hallelujah!
>   The message unto you I'll give;
> 'Tis recorded in His Word, hallelujah!
>   It is only that you "look and live."
> I will tell you how I came, hallelujah!
>   To Jesus when He made me whole:
> 'Twas believing on His name, hallelujah!
>   I trusted, and He saved my soul.

Poor Barabbas had followed the flesh. He had wasted a lifetime on the unimportant.

A story is told of a disastrous train wreck. A Christian engineer was dragged from the cab, bruised and badly crushed. In the hospital, when it was obvious that his injuries would soon prove fatal, his minister was called. The man, sensing the gravity of his condition, grasped his pastor by the hand and said with tears, *"Now that I am facing eternity, I realize I have lived all my life for secondary things!"*

That statement is true of so many. Many who have accepted Christ as Saviour are spending their lives on secondary things. Too many lukewarm believers have imbedded their roots too deeply in this passing world. Transient things demand so much attention that they leave to God only the dregs of a hurried, worried, fatigued life.

The man in cell number one

V. MIGHT HAVE BEEN SAVED

We do not know.

He was released. Jesus died in his place.

He might have trailed the cross to Calvary's hill. He might have watched them nail Jesus to the cross. He might have watched the suffering Saviour.

He might have heard the seven sayings of the cross: "Father, forgive them; for they know not what they do"; "Woman, behold thy son. Son, behold thy mother"; "To day shalt thou be with me in paradise"; "My God, my God, why hast thou forsaken me?"; "I thirst"; "It is finished"; "Father, into thy hands I commend my spirit."

When Jesus had uttered these words, He bowed His head upon His breast and breathed out His spirit. No one took His life from Him. He had power to lay it down of Himself.

Barabbas might have received the Man who died in his place.

The late John McNeill said that, of all the people in Jerusalem, he thought Barabbas had the best idea of the atonement of Jesus Christ.

Dr. McNeill put it in this fashion:

> You will remember that he should have been crucified and Jesus released. But the order was exactly reversed. The door of the prison swings open, and Barabbas is free.
> As he comes out into the light of the day, all the people seem

to be hurrying in one direction. He hears that Jesus of Nazareth is to be crucified. He stops a moment to think, then exclaims, "Why, that is the Man who is dying in my stead! I will go and see Him."

He pushes his way out through the gate of the city and up the hillside until he reaches the surging mob about the cross. He stands in the outer circle a moment, then pushes his way to the very inner circle and stands so near that he can reach out his hand and touch the dying Saviour. And I can hear him say, "I do not know who You are, but I know You are there in my stead."

And said John McNeill:

Until you can give a better theory of the atonement, take that of Barabbas—Christ your substitute, dying in your place.

Yes, Barabbas might have entered into new life in Christ Jesus. His eyes might have been turned from the things of this earth to the things of Heaven. He might have turned away from the dirt and filth of sinful man to the glory and purity of the eternal God.

Sam Hadley once said, "The night I was converted, I went out, looked up at the stars and thanked God for their beauty. I had not seen them for ten years. A drunkard never looks up."

A lot of folks miss the beauty of God. They do not see His workmanship. They do not understand His purpose. God grant that we might look up and have faith in Jesus Christ and know the God who loved us and sent His Son to die for us.

Let us close our thinking at this point, and let us make sure that we know the Christ of Calvary. Have you looked to Him for salvation? Have you made Him the Lord and Master of your life?

Let this be a moment of salvation, a time when you turn to the Lord Jesus. God grant that this might be the hour when you turn away from earthly things and center your affection and attention upon things eternal.

The Challenge of Mighty Prayer

"Then touched he their eyes, saying, According to your faith be it unto you."—Matt. 9:29.

"But Jesus beheld them, and said unto them, With men this is impossible; but with God all things are possible."—Matt. 19:26.

"Jesus said unto him, If thou canst believe, all things are possible to him that believeth."—Mark 9:23.

"Therefore I say unto you, What things soever ye desire, when ye pray, believe that ye receive them, and ye shall have them."— Mark 11:24.

Jesus said, "Men ought always to pray, and not to faint." Thank God for those things that make us pray! Thank God for those things that bring us to the end of our strength! Thank God for those things that make us see that only God has all power! Thank God that He loves us, cares for us and waits for our prayers!

I do pray. Scores and hundreds of my prayers have been definitely answered. But, oh, my failures! I confess my unfaithfulness in faithful, courageous praying. I confess that I hesitate to pray mighty prayers.

I am emphasizing in this message "mighty praying"—not just the returning of thanks at mealtimes, not just the habitual prayer at the close of the day, not just the formal prayer in the beginning of a worship hour on Sunday.

Give some thought to this theme: "The challenge of mighty prayer."

I. MIGHTY PRAYER RESTS ON SIMPLE FAITH

This is very plainly given to us in Mark 11:22-26, when Jesus said to His disciples, "What things soever ye desire, when ye pray, believe that ye receive them, and ye shall have them."

The great prayer warriors of the past were simple in faith. I refer to such names as George Mueller, "Praying Hyde," David Brainerd, Evan Roberts, John Wesley, George Whitefield, Jonathan Edwards, Adoniram Judson—just a few names that come to us as we think of mighty prayer warriors.

A little study of these men and their lives will reveal that great praying does not rest on education, on personality, on popularity or on wealth.

Great praying does not rest on position. The humblest Christian in our church can pray just as well as the most highly trained theologian or the highest official in the nation.

Our President-elect is receiving worldwide publicity, the new President of the world's strongest nation. But the humblest Christian in the hills of Tennessee can pray and get through to God just as quickly—and perhaps more quickly—than the President. It should not be true, but it is, that big people sometimes have much to hinder them in their prayer lives.

Simple faith! Jesus said to the disciples, "Have faith in God." On one occasion the disciples asked Jesus, "Lord, increase our faith." We need to pray in such a way in this time that our faith might be increased and that we might pray mighty prayers.

Prayer and faith will affect your appearance.

Prayer and faith will affect your personality.

Prayer and faith will affect your usefulness in the service of Christ.

Yes, mighty prayer rests on simple faith.

II. OFFER MIGHTY PRAYERS FOR OUR NEEDS

"But my God shall supply all your need according to his riches in glory by Christ Jesus."—Phil. 4:19.

"Ask, and it shall be given you; seek, and ye shall find; knock, and it shall be opened unto you: For every one that asketh receiveth; and he that seeketh findeth; and to him that knocketh it shall be opened."— Matt. 7:7,8.

We all have needs, so we should all pray—and pray about everything, the common, everyday needs of life.

Keep in mind that prevailing prayer is definite. It is not praying at random, not offering some prayer carelessly, but praying in a definite way for definite things.

First, let me say that mighty prayer is the God-ordained way for you to get what you need. Do you have financial needs? Then pray.

Be careful now that in the heart there is not a selfish intent.

That reminds me of a wife who kept coming to a revival meeting, asking that we pray for her husband. Prayer was offered for him by many people.

Finally he came to the service and was gloriously saved. The strange thing was, when he got saved, the wife quit coming to church altogether. She was confessing that her prayers had been selfish; and, of course, I do not think her prayers were answered, but the prayers of other faithful people were.

Beware of selfish praying!

Second, mighty prayer will make your testimony radiant. And the world needs glowing testimonies.

The difference in Christians is right here—some are gloomy, doubting and worried; others are trusting, faithful, happy and serving.

I was reading about Evan Roberts, the young man who preached so mightily and worked so faithfully in Scotland. One book I read told of his great joy in his work. One writer had this to say about him: "He seemed just bubbling over with sheer happiness— just as jubilant as a young man at a baseball game."

This young man had a radiant testimony, but he was a man who prayed "without ceasing." People came together in such numbers that there were no buildings in his country to seat them. They came into the auditorium in shifts; still many did not get inside. The blessings of God were upon the people. Souls were saved, lives were transformed.

Third, mighty prayer brings peace.

"Be careful for nothing; but in every thing by prayer and supplication with thanksgiving let your requests be made known unto God. And

the peace of God, which passeth all understanding, shall keep your hearts and minds through Christ Jesus."—Phil. 4:6,7.

A few hours ago I talked with a man from the Narramore Foundation. We talked about Dr. Clyde Narramore and about his great host of helpers. We discussed the Narramore Clinic and their plans for the future. This man said to me, "We have more people than we can care for. They come in such numbers that we cannot get around to all who want to be helped."

I appreciate what Dr. Narramore is doing; but, my dear friends, I believe that prayer will bring peace—mighty prayer, believing prayer, faithful prayer. If one prays, then the peace of God will fill his heart. When we pray and have peace, then there is no room for the worries and the anxieties that crowd in upon people. Paul is saying that here in Philippians 4: "Be careful for nothing; but in every thing by prayer and supplication with thanksgiving let your requests be made known unto God." When you pray like that, the "peace of God" will fill your hearts and lives.

III. OFFER MIGHTY PRAYERS FOR OTHERS

I am speaking now of intercessory prayer.

Samuel said, "God forbid that I should sin against the Lord in ceasing to pray for you: but I will teach you the good and the right way" (I Sam. 12:23).

Let us list a few of the ones for whom we should pray.

First, **for friends,** those who are near and dear to us. We should remember our families and our friends in fervent prayer. Not just the formal recitation of a few words in their behalf but agonizing unto God and asking for definite blessings on them.

Second, **for our enemies.** This is plainly what Jesus said in the Sermon on the Mount: "...and pray for them which despitefully use you, and persecute you" (Matt. 5:44). No one believes this is easy. This is the command of God given to those who have been born again by the Holy Spirit.

Again, **for the troubled.** Distressed souls are everywhere. Many folks are in the throes of great trouble. It is our part to remember them in prayer.

Again, **for the lost.** Make a prayer list for those who are lost in sin. I would like to feel that a few scores of you are praying every day for the salvation of the lost. It would be comforting to know that many of you pray earnestly before all of the services that God will bless and that souls will be saved.

Pray for people by name. Be concerned about the needs of others.

Someone has said, "The greatest thing a man can do for his Heavenly Father is to be kind to some of His other children."

That statement may need a little bit of interpretation. Yes, we should be kind to our fellow Christians, but we should also be kind to those who are lost in sin and seek to bring them to the Lord Jesus Christ. Prayer and kindness will certainly go together.

Will you begin to pray mightily in behalf of people? And don't get discouraged in your prayer life.

IV. MIGHTY PRAYER BRINGS MIRACLES

The story of Elijah is so well known that I need repeat but a portion of it. Elijah was a man with great faith in God. After a drought of more than three years, he showed himself to Ahab. Then he suggested that they have a contest on Mount Carmel.

The prophets of Baal came along and made their altar, and Elijah made his altar. The prophets of Baal prayed and prayed to their god, but nothing happened. Elijah mocked them. Then when it was time for Elijah to set up his altar, he took twelve stones according to the number of the tribes of the sons of Jacob and "built an altar in the name of the Lord."

He made a trench about the altar. He put the wood on, he cut the bullock in pieces and laid him on the wood, then said, "Fill four barrels with water, and pour it on the burnt sacrifice, and on the wood." It was done three times. The trench was filled with water, saturating the sacrifice.

Then Elijah the prophet came near to pray this prayer:

"...Lord God of Abraham, Isaac, and of Israel, let it be known this day that thou art God in Israel, and that I am thy servant, and that I have done all these things at thy word. Hear me, O Lord, hear me, *that this people may know that thou art the Lord God, and that thou hast turned their heart back again."*—I Kings 18:36, 37.

When the prayer was finished, the fire of the Lord fell and consumed the burnt sacrifice and the wood, the stones, the dust, and licked up the water that was in the trench.

Yes, mighty prayer brings miracles. Elijah's prayer was quite a contrast to the wild, monotonously repeated cry of the Baal worshipers.

"Wild cries and passionate desire flung upward to an unloved God are not prayers; and that solace, an anchor of the troubled soul, is wanting in all the dreary lands given up to idolatry."

But Elijah had a calm confidence in his God. He had a personal relationship to the Heavenly Father. He desired only that God might be glorified. Hence, he could pray and see great things happen.

Now, let us go back and take the verse that I read in Mark 9:23: "Jesus said unto him, If thou canst believe, all things are possible to him that believeth." Mighty prayers bring miracles.

What miracles do we need?

First, **the miracle of forgiveness.** My mind goes back to the sin of David. Nathan faced him with his sin. David repented and came back to God. He poured out his prayer unto the Lord in Psalm 51:1: "Have mercy upon me, O God, according to thy lovingkindness; according unto the multitude of thy tender mercies blot out my transgressions."

The prayer continues. David was forgiven. What a miracle of forgiveness! The holy God, the Creator of all things, comes down to forgive the sins of an humble believer.

We see the miracle of forgiveness also with regard to Simon Peter. He denied his Lord; then the cock crew. Peter went out and wept bitterly. We see the miracle of forgiveness.

Here is the promise that we need so very much: "If we confess our sins, he is faithful and just to forgive us our sins, and to cleanse us from all unrighteousness" (I John 1:9).

Second, **the miracle of usefulness.** Pray daily that God will use you. What a miracle that the Heavenly Father would stoop down to use poor, weak, faltering people. But He will. It may be as teacher, preacher, saint or witness; but God has a place for you and me.

Third, **the miracle of the Holy Spirit's power.** Prayer is an ingredient in obtaining spiritual power. Prayer is an essential in retaining Holy Spirit power. This has ever been true from Pentecost to the present time.

Fourth, **the miracle of great accomplishments.** Prayer can bring about the impossible. What we felt could never happen has been done by the blessed Lord in answer to fervent prayers.

V. MIGHTY PRAYER FOR COMPASSION

Our missionaries often turn to this portion of the Word of God, and it is right that they do so:

"And Jesus went about all the cities and villages, teaching in their synagogues, and preaching the gospel of the kingdom, and healing every sickness and every disease among the people.

"But when he saw the multitudes, he was moved with compassion on them, because they fainted, and were scattered abroad, as sheep having no shepherd.

"Then saith he unto his disciples, The harvest truly is plenteous, but the labourers are few;

"Pray ye therefore the Lord of the harvest, that he will send forth labourers into his harvest."—Matt. 9:35-38.

Jesus had compassion for people—for the sick, for the infirmed, but, most of all, for the souls of men.

What will bring compassion?

First, a study of the Word of God—not a critical study, but a reverential study. When in this Book we see the actions of our God in behalf of others, we cannot forget that He cares for and loves us.

Compassion is the keynote of the entire Bible. Perhaps the greatest thing that can be said about our God is that He is love. "He that loveth not knoweth not God; for God is love" (I John 4:8).

Second, seeking for Christlikeness will bring compassion. Seek to walk in the steps of your Master. Every day try to emulate Him in His love for others.

A father and son were standing on the top of a hill. The father

was pointing out various parts of the landscape to the east and to
the west, to the north and to the south. Then, finally sweeping his
hand and eye all around the encircling horizon, he said, "My son,
God's love is as big as all that!"

The boy answered with great faith and happiness, "Then, Father,
we must be in the middle of it!"

Third, an observation of man's need will bring compassion. We
must see the lost condition of men and understand what it means
to be lost and Hell-bound. We must see the helplessness of man, the
downward course on which he is traveling and reach out to help that
one.

Finally, fervent prayers will bring compassion. Openly ask for
what you need. If you need compassion of heart, then ask for it.

Last Monday evening quite late, a man called and asked if he
might talk to me for a few minutes. I told him that I had already
gone to bed and would prefer to see him the next day. I asked him
if he was saved. "Yes, I am a Christian, but I must talk to you."

I made an appointment to see him the next day. I found that he
was a preacher of the Gospel. We got in his car and began driving.
He drove me out to his church field. Finally, he broke down and said,
"I do want you to pray for me. I do want God's help. I have lost all
my compassion for the souls of men. One day I had it, but not now.
I cannot go on unless I regain that compassion for the souls of men."

We had a prayer together, and I made certain suggestions. I trust
that what I said will be helpful.

We must have compassion of soul that will help us to bring others
to the Lord Jesus Christ.

The One Act That Touches All Eternity

"For she said within herself, If I may but touch his garment, I shall be whole."—Matt. 9:21.

There is a sense in which everything touches all eternity.

A kind word may influence a life, and the power of that life may touch others—for eternity.

A generous act may touch eternity. The little woman giving the two mites had no idea that her humble deed would be recorded in the infallible Word of God and stand forever.

An act of bravery may touch all eternity. It might be the rescuing of someone from a burning building or the saving of a life from drowning.

In like manner, negative acts touch others and, hence, touch eternity.

The drunken father leads his children to drunkenness. He turns his own away from God to the sins of this world. The worldly mother influences her children for evil. They follow her and become as she is.

Paul said in Romans 14:7, "For none of us liveth to himself, and no man dieth to himself."

Every person has an influence for good or evil. The apostle exhorts us to carefulness in living.

A few days ago I conducted the funeral of a lad eighteen years of age. The boy had made a profession of faith in Christ at twelve years of age. He obeyed the Lord in baptism. I mentioned to the family and friends that that single act of his life touched all eternity.

By one act of life, a boy of twelve touched the throne of God.

By one act of life, a boy of twelve caused the angel to write his name in the Lamb's Book of Life.

By one act of life, a boy of twelve closed forever the doorway of Hell to his own soul.

By that one act of life, a boy of twelve had Heaven opened to him.

Jesus said, "Verily, verily, I say unto you, He that believeth on me hath everlasting life" (John 6:47).

Here is the one act that touches all eternity.

I. THE ACT IS PERSONAL

There is no such thing as a secondhand faith. It is personal or nothing.

We may wear another's clothes or shoes, but we cannot possess another's saving faith. It must be personal.

We can live in another's house, but we must have our own faith.

It cannot be inherited from parents, grandparents or friends.

We can get much from others, but our faith must be our own; individually, we must trust Christ.

How often I have tried to deal with children or young people in a home where the mother tried to give all the answers. When I questioned a young man about his salvation, she would try to insert the answers for her son.

Not so! Every person must answer for himself. The Bible bears this out, as in the accounts of Nicodemus, Zacchaeus, Stephen, Cornelius and the jailor. Each had to answer for himself.

Have you come face to face with Christ? Have you received Him? No one can answer for you. This is your decision.

What monumental things happen when, by the single act of faith, we receive Jesus Christ as Saviour. Let us keep before us such a verse as John 1:12, "But as many as received him, to them gave he power to become the sons of God, even to them that believe on his name."

First, by the single act of receiving Christ, you become a child of God. By the act of faith, you have a new name, a new purpose, a new direction. You belong to God's family (Eph. 3:15).

Second, a storehouse of provisions is opened unto you. Paul said in Philippians 4:19, "But my God shall supply all your need according to his riches in glory by Christ Jesus."

In Matthew 6:25-34, the Lord told His disciples—and us—that we have but one task—to seek first the kingdom of God; then all things will be added unto us.

The child of God has everything provided for his daily needs.

Third, when you become a child of God, the Bible is your guidebook. The sinner cannot understand this Bible. The apostle said, "But the natural man receiveth not the things of the Spirit of God: for they are foolishness unto him: neither can he know them, because they are spiritually discerned" (I Cor. 2:14).

The Bible is a closed book for that one who knows not Christ.

Have you accepted Him as your Saviour? It is not a matter of your family or of your friends: this is a personal matter. Have **you** put your faith in Christ? Are **you** trusting Him to save you and take you to Heaven?

II. THE ACT IS PERMANENT

"And I give unto them eternal life; and they shall never perish, neither shall any man pluck them out of my hand."—John 10:28.

"For the which cause I also suffer these things: nevertheless I am not ashamed: for I know whom I have believed, and am persuaded that he is able to keep that which I have committed unto him against that day."—II Tim. 1:12.

The Bible declares that we are saved by grace:

"For by grace are ye saved through faith; and that not of yourselves: it is the gift of God: Not of works, lest any man should boast."—Eph. 2:8,9.

The Bible says that we are saved eternally:

"Verily, verily, I say unto you, He that heareth my word, and believeth on him that sent me, hath everlasting life, and shall not come into condemnation; but is passed from death unto life."—John 5:24.

In a fluctuating, changing world—this is permanent! When you put your faith in Christ, your salvation is as secure as God Himself.

Why? Because you have His Word: "Heaven and earth shall pass away, but my words shall not pass away" (Matt. 24:35).

Some years ago I published a little booklet entitled *Ten Reasons Why I Believe in Once Saved, Always Saved.* These are the ten reasons that I gave:

1. Salvation is a gift: "For the wages of sin is death; but the gift of God is eternal life through Jesus Christ our Lord" (Rom. 6:23).

2. Salvation establishes a relationship: "Beloved, now are we the sons of God, and it doth not yet appear what we shall be: but we know that when he shall appear, we shall be like him; for we shall see him as he is" (I John 3:2).

3. This relationship is eternal: "And this is the will of him that sent me, that every one which seeth the Son, and believeth on him, may have everlasting life: and I will raise him up at the last day" (John 6:40).

4. This salvation depends upon the finished work of Christ: "And as Moses lifted up the serpent in the wilderness, even so must the Son of man be lifted up" (John 3:14). "When Jesus therefore had received the vinegar, he said, It is finished: and he bowed his head, and gave up the ghost" (John 19:30).

5. The requirement for salvation is made plain in the Word of God: "He that believeth on the Son hath everlasting life: and he that believeth not the Son shall not see life; but the wrath of God abideth on him" (John 3:36).

6. The Christian's sins affect his fellowship but not his relationship. There are two words that every Christian should know: *relationship* and *fellowship.* We are brought into the family of God when we receive Jesus Christ by faith. This relationship is eternal. Our mistakes and failures affect our fellowship but not our relationship. Read carefully the following in I John 1:8-2:1:

"If we say that we have no sin, we deceive ourselves, and the truth is not in us.

"If we confess our sins, he is faithful and just to forgive us our sins, and to cleanse us from all unrighteousness.

"If we say that we have not sinned, we make him a liar, and his word is not in us.

"My little children, these things write I unto you, that ye sin not. And if any man sin, we have an advocate with the Father, Jesus Christ the righteous."

7. The Christian is sealed by the Holy Spirit.

"In whom ye also trusted, after that ye heard the word of truth, the gospel of your salvation: in whom also after that ye believed, ye were sealed with that holy Spirit of promise."—Eph. 1:13.

"And grieve not the holy Spirit of God, whereby ye are sealed unto the day of redemption."—Eph. 4:30.

8. God has promised that nothing can separate us from Him:

"Who shall lay anything to the charge of God's elect? It is God that justifieth.

"Who is he that condemneth? It is Christ that died, yea rather, that is risen again, who is even at the right hand of God, who also maketh intercession for us.

"Who shall separate us from the love of Christ? shall tribulation, or distress, or persecution, or famine, or nakedness, or peril, or sword?

"As it is written, For thy sake we are killed all the day long; we are accounted as sheep for the slaughter.

"Nay, in all these things we are more than conquerors through him that loved us.

"For I am persuaded, that neither death, nor life, nor angels, nor principalities, nor powers, nor things present, nor things to come,

"Nor height, nor depth, nor any other creature, shall be able to separate us from the love of God, which is in Christ Jesus our Lord."—Rom. 8:33-39.

9. Paul says that there is no condemnation: "There is therefore now no condemnation to them which are in Christ Jesus, who walk not after the flesh, but after the Spirit" (Rom. 8:1).

10. Jesus' promise that He will preserve the relationship: "All that the Father giveth me shall come to me; and him that cometh

to me I will in no wise cast out" (John 6:37).

Shout the praises of God that the salvation given unto us by faith is permanent! The entire Bible stands back of this great truth. Your salvation is dependent upon your faith in the eternal Christ. When by personal faith you enter into the family of God, then you abide in that relationship forever. God's children are chastened, but they are not cast out. Read carefully Hebrews 12:3-15.

III. THE ACT IS PERSUASIVE

There was a day when the Apostle Paul stood before Agrippa. He gave the Gospel in all of its purity. He told of the coming of the Lord Jesus Christ and of the manifestation of the Saviour to him on the road to Damascus. The simple and mighty words poured from the lips of the apostle. Paul said to King Agrippa, ". . . believest thou the prophets? I know that thou believest" (Acts 26:27). "Then Agrippa said unto Paul, Almost thou persuadest me to be a Christian" (vs. 28).

The life and testimony of Paul touched this one and "almost persuaded" him to come to Christ.

My life touches another. This is God's way. We are to touch others by word and by influence.

My acceptance of Christ touched all eternity—it meant my salvation.

My acceptance of Christ means also that I am to touch others by showing forth Christ and by the proclamation of the message of Christ. I am to "go" with the Gospel.

We are back to the theme of helping others.

The disciples were saved and charged to go out and preach. This they did.

Stephen was saved and charged to tell others. This he did. His message touched the heart of Saul of Tarsus.

Philip was saved and commissioned to tell others. God sent him from a flourishing revival in Samaria, down into the desert country to the Ethiopian to tell him about Jesus Christ.

Paul was saved; and "straightway he preached Christ in the synagogues, that he is the Son of God" (Acts 9:20).

God's ordained way for the spread of the Gospel is that we live out Christ and preach Him everywhere. The purpose of our visitation and preaching programs is that we might present the message and persuade men to repent and believe.

David B. Stewart wrote these lines about the young Scottish preacher, Robert Murray McCheyne:

> He left his mark as few have done
>   On history's golden page.
> The record of his holy life
>   Has meaning for our age.
>
> Oh, give us, Lord, concrete desire
> To be like him, a soul on fire.
>
> At Calvary he found the love
>   Which drew his heart away
> From all the emptiness of life,
>   Its glitter and array.
>
> His life, transformed, would henceforth show
> The debt of love which he did owe.
>
> And still our God can work today
>   If we but seek His face
> For mighty movements of His love,
>   Outpourings of His grace.
>
> McCheyne-like, let our spirits weep
> That God would find the long lost sheep.

Three thoughts I would like to press upon your hearts and minds at this time.

First, **salvation is redemptive.** We have been bought with a price—the precious blood of the Lord Jesus.

> Nor silver nor gold hath obtained my redemption,
>   Nor riches of earth could have saved my poor soul;
> The blood of the cross is my only foundation,
>   The death of my Saviour now maketh me whole.
>
> Nor silver nor gold hath obtained my redemption,
>   The way into Heaven could not thus be bought;
> The blood of the cross is my only foundation,
>   The death of my Saviour redemption hath wrought.

We have been redeemed by the blood of the Lord Jesus.

Charles G. Finney used to tell of a lawyer who received Christ as his Saviour. Upon doing so, he executed a formal deed in full legal terminology by which he conveyed himself, his powers and his possessions to God.

This is good. We are not our own. We have been bought with a price.

Second, **salvation is transforming**: "Therefore if any man be in Christ, he is a new creature: old things are passed away; behold, all things are become new" (II Cor. 5:17). We are changed and transformed—made new—by the power of God!

Third, **salvation is to be shared.** Tell the whole world is God's plan.

Think for a moment of the three points to the message of this evening. We have been discussing "The One Act That Changes All Eternity." First, the act is personal. Second, the act is permanent. Third, the act is persuasive. Be sure that your salvation has all three of these characteristics.

Your salvation should touch others. We are not to be secret disciples, like Nicodemus and Joseph of Arimathea; but we are to help others to know Christ, be proclaimers of His message.

Salvation is the work of God! It is costly—God gave His only Son! It is serious and meaningful! God grant that we might see and understand that our acceptance of Jesus Christ as Saviour is the one act that touches all of time.

Joan Collins told the story about the leader of the church in Chad. The work had been experiencing some difficulties, and the native leader of this work wrote two missionaries and expressed his unswerving loyalty to the cause of Christ. He said, "If I had ten pairs of hands, they would all serve Jesus Christ. If I had ten pairs of feet, they would all be used to go with the message of salvation to others."

Someone put the thought into poetry:

> **If I had ten lives to give Thee,**
> **Ten hearts to love Thee well,**
> **Ten minds to think thoughts of Thee,**
> **Ten mouths Thy grace to tell,**

Lord, I would give them gladly
To show my love to Thee;
For Jesus, by His precious blood,
Stooped down and saved e'en me.

But I have only one life to offer,
One heart with which to love,
One mind to reason with Thee,
One soul destined for above.

Then take this life I offer,
And use me, Lord, e'en me,
To show Thy love to others
And bring much praise to Thee.

What Is Your Goal in Life?

"For the Son of man is come to seek and to save that which was lost."—Luke 19:10.

"Pilate therefore said unto him, Art thou a king then? Jesus answered, Thou sayest that I am a king. To this end was I born, and for this cause came I into the world, that I should bear witness unto the truth. Every one that is of the truth heareth my voice."—John 18:37.

"This is a faithful saying, and worthy of all acceptation, that Christ Jesus came into the world to save sinners; of whom I am chief."—I Tim. 1:15.

Discouragement often comes because we do not set a goal for our lives. Or we may become discouraged because we have temporarily lost sight of the goal.

What is your goal, your aim and purpose in life?

If you answer none, then I can quickly say that your life will be wasted. To achieve anything worthwhile, one must aim in a definite direction.

Moses had a goal. It was to lead the people out of Egypt. Through many hardships and trials he persisted. Their disobedience and unwillingness did not deter him. He continued until he had them in sight of the Promised Land.

Joshua had a goal. It was to lead the people into Canaan land and to conquer the cities.

Solomon had a goal. It was to build the Temple. Solomon's troubles did not begin until after the Temple was built. It is then that Solomon loved many strange women, and his heart was turned away after other gods, and his heart was not perfect toward the Lord his God (I Kings 11:1,4).

Nehemiah had a goal. It was to rebuild the walls of Jerusalem. Opposition came against him, but he continued until the job was completed.

Elijah had a goal. It was to obey God and to turn the hearts of the people back to God.

John the Baptist had a goal. It was to be the forerunner of Christ and to point out the Saviour.

The Apostle Paul had a goal. It was to do the will of God. And that will was for Paul to bear the name of Christ before Gentiles, kings and the children of Israel. Paul could say of his life, "For to me to live is Christ."

The Lord Jesus had a goal, stated in the verses at the beginning of the message. Christ came to seek and to save that which was lost. He came to bear witness unto the truth, and He was the Truth.

Do you have a goal? If so, is it a worthy one?

May we briefly examine what a goal should be.

I. A GOAL SHOULD BE SCRIPTURAL

Perhaps you are saying now, "The goal of my life is to do this or that." Examine your goal in the light of the Bible. Does the Word of God give approval of that which you have decided to do with your life?

Remember the Word of God is against selfishness. If your goal is selfish, then it is not scriptural.

The Word of God is against impurity. If the goal of your life ignores the Bible standard of purity, then it is an unworthy goal.

The Word of God is against drunkenness. If the goal of your life does not lead to sobriety and uprightness, it is not scriptural.

The Word of God is against dishonesty. If your goal is to be reached by dishonest methods, then God is against that.

The Word of God is against laziness. Therefore, if the goal of your life does not include faithful, hard work, then it is not scriptural.

If you are simply aiming at having an easy time in life, the Word of God does not commend you.

May I illustrate?

Saul and Barnabas were members of the church in Antioch. They were leaders in the work, but both had one great goal—to please God. Therefore, when the Holy Spirit said, "Separate me Barnabas and Saul for the work whereunto I have called them," they were willing to do what the Spirit said. They launched into a missionary journey. Their mission was to take the Gospel to as many people as possible. They were not seeking for money or for luxury, but simply to do the will of God.

Now, if we examine their goal in the light of the Scripture, what do we find?

First, they were following in the steps of Jesus Christ, who came to seek and to save that which was lost.

Second, they were not setting forth upon a journey for selfish reasons. There is no indication that any return came to these men for their service.

Third, as we examine their goal, we see that it was true to the Great Commission; for Christ has commanded us to go into all the world and preach the Gospel to every creature.

Therefore, take your goal and examine it in the light of the Bible. Perhaps your goal is to make money. Daily you give yourself to the acquiring of this world's goods. Then you had better ask yourself, "For what purpose?" If it is simply to get ahead of others or to make a name for yourself or to live in selfishness, then your goal is not according to the Word of God.

II. OUR GOAL SHOULD CHALLENGE US

No goal is worthwhile that does not challenge you to do and to give your best. Your goal should consume your entire interest and be a guiding light in every day's activity.

A goal should be big enough to challenge you all of your days. It should always be ahead of you, yet daily it can be touched and reached in part.

Paul had a goal for the winning of the lost. Each day the goal was touched, yet it was always ahead. Still, he so worked at the goal that, when he came to the end of the way, he could feel that he had achieved the end for which Christ had saved him.

I mentioned Solomon and his goal to build the Temple in Jerusalem. His was a worthy goal. It had been denied his father David, but with great wisdom Solomon gathered together materials and workmen, and the Temple was built. The dedication day came, and Solomon offered one of the great prayers recorded in the Bible, a prayer of humility and thanksgiving that the Temple was finished.

Solomon had reached his goal; then sin entered in. His heart was turned away from God, and he did evil in the sight of the Lord. Therefore, we can only conclude that Solomon's goal was not big enough, not of such nature to challenge him all the days of his life.

A small goal is a handicap.

Suppose you had set a goal to own your own home. This was all that you had in mind. Therefore, you buy a house and begin paying on it. You work and slave for one purpose—to own your own home, to have the security of your own property.

Within a few years this goal is reached; then at once your life begins to deteriorate.

Let your goal be big enough to challenge you all the days of your life.

Joshua succeeded greatly in the work that God gave him to do; but when he laid down the work at 110 years of age, God said, "There remaineth yet very much land to be possessed" (Josh. 13:1). He had touched the fringe of the garment of the goal, but it was still ahead of him.

Paul succeeded in his ministry, but he counted not himself to have apprehended but reached forth to the things that are before.

America today needs a goal. We need leadership that can give us a challenge for a great goal, an aim, a purpose. In war days this nation moved forward with unity and solidarity. We had a goal, we were aiming at something. But in such a time as this, we face great danger because we are not aiming at some specific goal.

Oh, for a vision that challenges! Sunday schools grow when they have goals before them. At a Sunday school convention some days ago a man gave this outline for growing a great Sunday school:

First, envision. See the field white unto harvest.

Second, enlarge. Make room to reach greater numbers.

Third, energize. Put your plans to work.

Fourth, enlist. Get others interested in reaching the goal.

Fifth, endure—that is, be persistent in the work.

In the building of a great church, there must be a goal; and as far as I am concerned, that goal must be the winning of the lost. A goal that should steady and challenge us is always seeking the lost.

Choose a goal for your life. And make sure that goal challenges you to give your best. Be definite in the goal. Don't waver. Look to a definite destination.

When I was a boy, my father gave me this advice about riding in a car: "Never get in a car without a destination." Good advice. Trouble comes when you are just riding around with no aim, no destination.

III. A GOAL SHOULD GLORIFY GOD

The goal that disregards the claims of God upon your life is wrong. The goal that does not lift up the Lord before others is unworthy.

If your goal takes you away from prayer, the Bible, church attendance, soul winning and other Christian activities, it is wrong. If your goal leads you into dishonesty, immorality or low living, then it does not glorify God and is unworthy.

The Bible tells us how we can glorify God.

We should glorify God in our good works:

"Let your light so shine before men, that they may see your good works, and glorify your Father which is in heaven."—Matt. 5:16.

We can glorify God in bearing fruit:

"Herein is my Father glorified, that ye bear much fruit; so shall ye be my disciples."—John 15:8.

We can glorify God by complete consecration:

"For ye are bought with a price: therefore glorify God in your body, and in your spirit, which are God's."—I Cor. 6:20.

Christ ever sought to glorify the Heavenly Father. Note these verses in the Gospel of John:

"Therefore, when he was gone out, Jesus said, Now is the Son of man glorified, and God is glorified in him. If God be glorified in him, God shall also glorify him in himself, and shall straightway glorify him."—John 13:31,32.

In the matter of prayer Jesus said,

"And whatsoever ye shall ask in my name, that will I do, that the Father may be glorified in the Son."—John 14:13.

In the great prayer of Jesus as recorded in John 17, we find Him saying,

"I have glorified thee on the earth: I have finished the work which thou gavest me to do."—Vs. 4.

Make sure your life is glorifying God, whether it be in the business or religious world.

IV. A GOAL SHOULD CONSIDER OTHERS

No goal is right that disregards the interests of others. The man was wrong who said, "I am going to the top—I don't care whom I hurt getting there." This is not the spirit of Christ, and it will bring loss to any life.

> **Others, Lord, yes, others,**
> **Let this my motto be;**
> **Help me to live for others**
> **That I may live for Thee.**

As a Christian, let your goal be considerate of those immediately around you. Is your life a blessing to them? Are you being helpful to them?

Your goal should also consider those in uttermost parts of the earth—that is, missions.

Make money? Yes—but use it for the winning of lost souls.

Be a civic leader? Yes—but use your leadership to point others to the Saviour.

Be an executive? Yes—but use your ability and position to

lead others to the Lord Jesus Christ.

Be a great musician? Yes—but use it to lead men to the Saviour.

One goal every person should have is the winning of men to Christ. This goal will challenge us and give purpose to our daily living. It will keep us close to the Lord, make us consistent in our life, give us cause for rejoicing and burden our heart.

Some years ago the New York Fire Department had a great parade. One feature was three buses loaded with people from all walks of life, the high and the low. Signs on these buses read:

ALL OF THESE WERE SAVED BY OUR FIRE DEPARTMENT
FROM BURNING BUILDINGS.

As we look back, can we think of many whom we had part in leading to the Lord Jesus through our testimony and in saving from an eternal Hell? This should ever be our consuming passion. In this God will be glorified.

A Decisive Decade

". . . Father, if thou be willing, remove this cup from me: nevertheless not my will, but thine, be done."—Luke 22:42.

We just completed a decade of work in Tennessee Temple Schools. It has been a decisive decade!

It has been a decade of progress—progress in enrollment, in buildings, in curriculum and in our teaching staff.

It has been a decade of problems. Some know more about this than others. Sometimes the problems have been financial; at other times, administrative. But in every problem, God has shown His hand and given His leadership.

It has been a decade of peace. Peace comes through obedience to His will. There may be problems, decisions and dilemmas; but peace comes when we resign all to Him.

Tennessee Temple Schools had its beginning in my heart. There was given to me a vision of a school which would do the work which Tennessee Temple is now doing. I had no anticipation of the extent to which this work might go, but I had a willingness for God to lead.

The name, Tennessee Temple Schools, was given to me in answer to prayer. I know not how the name came into my mind, but I do know that God was back of it.

Now the question, Why did we begin Tennessee Temple Schools? Was it to make a name? No. Was it to hurt someone else? No. Was it to show our independence of a denomination? No.

Tennessee Temple began with a definite purpose of getting the

Gospel out to lost people. That is still our aim. To this end we send missionaries around the world. They labor tonight on fields which circle the globe—in Africa, Central America, the West Indies, South America, Italy, Mexico, among the Jewish people, Canada, Japan and in many other places. We rejoice that God has given us a part in sending the Gospel to the ends of the earth.

Not only are our graduates working as missionaries, but many are also successful pastors and evangelists.

Still others are workers in various fields, such as assistant pastors, educational directors, church secretaries and teachers.

Now, what has been the motivating purpose in all of this work? I put it under three headings:

I. TO GLORIFY HIS NAME

It was Jesus who said, "Father, glorify thy name."

The Son of God had a desire to glorify the Father's name. This desire should be the desire of every child of God.

What do the men of this world want? Self-glory. What do they desire? Ease and pleasure.

What should we desire? To glorify His name. A forgetting of self and of selfish desires. A denial of self. A turning from the leadership of the world.

When a man says, "I am going to seek the will of God and endeavor to glorify the name of the Heavenly Father," what he is planning to do may seem foolish; but if this is his desire, I can understand it at least in part.

But when a man openly says, "I believe that, if I walk along with others, it will mean more advancement for me in the world"—such an attitude I cannot understand. No desire to glorify the Father's name but a turning to instead of a turning away from the leadership of the world.

By all means, friend, seek to glorify His name. This will mean a denial of self, a forgetting of selfish pleasures and a turning from the affairs of this world.

II. OUR MOTIVATING PURPOSE—TO GIVE THE
SAVING GOSPEL OF JESUS CHRIST
TO LOST MEN EVERYWHERE

Anton Andersen, veteran missionary of the Congo Gospel Mission, went to be with the Lord. Two of his sons, Fred and Elward, are graduates of Tennessee Temple Schools. Brother Andersen spent over forty years in the Congo, laboring night and day as a faithful missionary. At his Homegoing, thousands of natives walked by the casket to view the body. And thousands attended the funeral service.

He died leaving no personal property. A member of the family has written to us that perhaps the only piece of property he left was a broken-down tractor. This he had used in plowing the gardens for those who helped him in his work.

He is buried in Africa where he wanted to be buried. Forty years spent on one field! Forty years well spent in the winning of precious souls to the Saviour! Forty years well spent if only one heathen had been saved!

Was his life noble? Yes, more than noble—blessed. Not many people know about the death of Anton Andersen in our country; but in the heavenly realms, many will rise up to call him blessed because this soul winner told them the story of Jesus Christ.

Give the saving Gospel to the lost. Magnify the message of our Lord. Tell men that Christ died for sinners. Determine to give this Word to all men. Repeat it, for they hear so poorly. Men hear what they want to hear, and the world is pressing in upon them at such a speed that they fail to hear the message of Christ.

That Christ died for sinners is the message which must be brought to the ears of sinners everywhere.

The story is told of the troubled days in Scotland. Sir John Cochrane was condemned to die by the king. The death warrant was on its way.

Sir John Cochrane was bidding farewell to his daughter Grizelle at the prison door: "Farewell, my child. I must die."

His daughter said, "No, Father, you shall not die!"

"But," he said, "the king is against me, the law is after me, and the death warrant is on its way. I must die. Do not deceive yourself, my dear child."

The daughter said, "Father, you shall not die!" as she left the prison door.

That night on the moors of Scotland a disguised wayfarer stood waiting for the horseman carrying the mailbags containing the death warrant.

As the horse came by, the wayfarer clutched the bridle and shouted to the rider, "Dismount!" The rider felt for his arms and was about to shoot, but the wayfarer jerked him from his saddle, and he fell flat. The wayfarer picked up the mailbags, put them on his shoulder and vanished in the darkness. Fourteen days were thus gained for the prisoner's life.

The second time the death warrant is on its way. The disguised wayfarer comes along, stops at an inn to get a bite to eat, then goes on out into the night. Finally he stopped in the brambles and waited for the horseman to come carrying the mail containing the death warrant of Sir John Cochrane.

The mail carrier spurred on his steed, for he was fearful because of what had occurred on the former journey. Suddenly through the storm and darkness there was a flash of firearms. The horse became unmanageable. As the mail carrier discharged his pistol in response, the horse threw him. The wayfarer put his foot on the breast of the overthrown rider and demanded, "Surrender now!"

The mail carrier surrendered his arms, and the disguised wayfarer put upon his shoulders the mailbags, leaped upon his horse and sped away into the darkness, gaining fourteen more days for the poor prisoner, Sir John Cochrane.

Before the fourteen days had expired, a pardon had come from the king. The door of the prison swung open, and Sir John Cochrane was free.

One day when he was standing amid his friends who were congratulating him, the disguised wayfarer appeared at the gate. Sir John Cochrane said, "Admit him right away."

The disguised wayfarer came in and said, "Here are two letters. Read them, Sir."

Sir John Cochrane read them—his two death warrants. He turned and threw them into the fire, then said, "To whom am I indebted, and who is this poor wayfarer who saved my life? Who is he?"

The wayfarer pulled away the cloak, the coat and the hat. Who was it? Grizelle, the daughter of Sir John Cochrane!

The Word of God says, "The soul that sinneth it shall die." The death warrant has been given. We must die! But breasting the storm comes a Wayfarer who grips by the bridle the oncoming doom and swings it back. Meanwhile, the pardon flashes from the throne, "Go free! Open the gate! You have been made free in Jesus Christ!"

The message we want men to hear is that the Saviour died upon the cross that sinners might have salvation.

III. OUR MOTIVATING PURPOSE BACK OF THIS WORK— TO DO THE WILL OF GOD

The picture is clear in Luke 22. Christ went into the Garden. He knelt down and prayed, "Father, if thou be willing, remove this cup from me: nevertheless not my will, but thine, be done."

Was the struggle real? Oh, yes. See the angel coming down from Heaven. Jesus prayed in great agony until blood fell from His body to the ground.

It will be a real struggle for you. The world, the flesh and the Devil will seek the ascendancy. Stay with the fight! Follow the Lord Jesus and surrender all unto Him.

A new day begins for you—a new day in your Christian experience when you surrender all to the Son of God. Your will must be put down that His will might be done. There is always a struggle, yes, a contest; but determine that He will have His way.

Talmage used to tell the story of the boy named Stewart Holland. It is said that a vessel crashed into the Arctic in a fog. When it was found that the ship must go down, some of the passengers got into the lifeboat, some got on rafts; but three hundred went to the bottom.

During all those hours of calamity, Stewart Holland stood at the signal gun and sounded it across the sea. The helmsman forsook his place, the engineer was gone. Some fainted, some prayed, some blasphemed. The powder had been used up, so they could not let off the signal gun again. But the lad broke into the magazine, brought out more powder, and again the gun boomed over the sea.

Let this story have two applications: first, determine to let God have His way and that you will do the work that He has assigned unto you; second, give the signal out to others. Warn them of death and judgment. Tell them that now is the accepted time; be saved today. Warn men of the wrath to come and the awfulness of Hell. Tell men of the tender, outstretched arms of our Saviour, waiting to receive all who will come to Him.

God grant tonight that some of you will determine to be different, that you will turn away from the average excuse-making type of Christian and let God have His way. Let your motto be GOD FIRST! Seek to glorify His name. Give to lost men the saving Gospel of Christ. And do the will of God.

Will the way be easy? By no means. There will be hardships, heartaches, loneliness. But in it all will be the peace that comes by doing the will of God.

Hear Jesus as He speaks, 'Not My will, but Thine, be done.' See the angel as he appeared from Heaven and came to Him and strengthened Him.

God never forgets His own. In the time of greatest trial, He will give sustenance and aid.

The Fountain of Youth

"Jesus answered and said unto her, If thou knewest the gift of God, and who it is that saith to thee, Give me to drink; thou wouldest have asked of him, and he would have given thee living water.

"Jesus answered and said unto her, Whosoever drinketh of this water shall thirst again:

"But whosoever drinketh of the water that I shall give him shall never thirst; but the water that I shall give him shall be in him a well of water springing up into everlasting life."—John 4:10,13,14.

The Spanish explorer, Ponce de Leon, searched for the Fountain of Youth. In 1513 he secured three ships and set out to find a curative fountain. His journey brought him to the part of our country known today as Florida. It was Ponce de Leon who gave it this name.

The famed explorer failed to find the Fountain of Youth because he looked in the wrong places. Had he searched in a Book—the Bible—he could have found therein the true Fountain of Eternal Youth.

Had Ponce de Leon read such words as these, "But whosoever drinketh of the water that I shall give him shall never thirst," his longing soul could have been satisfied in Jesus Christ.

Or he might have read these words: "If any man thirst, let him come unto me, and drink. He that believeth on me, as the scripture hath said, out of his belly shall flow rivers of living water" (John 7:37,38).

Again, Ponce de Leon might have read the closing invitation in the Bible, as found in Revelation 22:17, "And the Spirit and the bride say, Come. And let him that heareth say, Come. And let him that is athirst come. And whosoever will, let him take the water of life freely."

Christ is that Fountain of Life, Giver of the water of life to all men.

Follow me in three simple statements about the water that Christ gives.

I. IT IS PURE, NOT POLLUTED

The Fountain of Life in Christ is pure, not polluted; fresh, not foul. The world is filled with fountains which are impure. These fountains will increase the impurity of an already depraved mankind.

When I was a boy in Louisville, Kentucky, we were notified of the serious illness of my grandmother. We quickly went to southern Indiana, the home place of my father. In a short time my grandmother expired. As I recall it now, another member of our family died about the same time.

We returned to Louisville after the funeral, and I became ill with typhoid fever. Many people who attended the funeral service also became sick with typhoid.

After awhile someone began to try to find out why so many people became ill. Someone suggested that it was because of the well at the old home place. Finally, the well was cleaned out, and in the bottom was found a dead rat. Here was the cause for the illness and death of my grandmother and another member of the family, plus the illness of many.

So it is with fountains of this world. They are impure and contain death-dealing germs.

We long for that which is pure and fresh—fresh air, fresh water, fresh flowers, fresh experiences. We make a mistake when we try to find freshness in a dirty, vile world.

There is only one unfailing source of freshness, and that is in Christ Himself. Are you not aware of the freshness of Christ when you come to the place of prayer and talk with Him? Are you not aware that the words of Christ are always fresh?

The old, familiar words of our Saviour never lose their freshness whether we are reading the plan of salvation as given in John 3:16 or reading the words of the Master as He said, "Come unto me, all ye that labour and are heavy laden." There is a freshness and a beauty about every word of our Saviour.

Let us resolve to turn from that which is impure and foul. Our Christ had no part in impurity and filth. He bids us to take into our lives that which is clean and life-giving. The Word says, "Abhor that which is evil, cleave to that which is good."

The Apostle Paul tells us that we are to think upon the things which are pure and good:

"Finally, brethren, whatsoever things are true, whatsoever things are honest, whatsoever things are just, whatsoever things are pure, whatsoever things are lovely, whatsoever things are of good report; if there be any virtue, and if there be any praise, think on these things."— Phil. 4:8.

A beautiful and touching story of David fighting against the Philistines is given in II Samuel 23. They were garrisoned in Bethlehem, and it is written, "David longed, and said, Oh that one would give me drink of the water of the well of Bethlehem, which is by the gate!"

Three of his mighty men broke through the army of the Philistines, drew water out of the well and brought it to David. Though David longed for it, he refused to drink it because they had brought it to him at the risk of their own lives. He poured it out as an offering unto the Lord.

The emphasis of the story is that we long for that which is clean, fresh and pure. We will find the satisfaction for our longing hearts in Jesus Christ, the Giver of the water of life.

II. THE WATER THAT CHRIST GIVES IS ALWAYS INCREASING, NOT DIMINISHING

Christ said, "But the water that I shall give him shall be in him a well of water, springing up into everlasting life." He said, "He that believeth on me, as the scripture hath said, out of his belly shall flow rivers of living water."

The world is filled with failing fountains and broken cisterns.

Jeremiah told the backslidden people of Israel, "For my people have committed two evils; they have forsaken me, the fountain of living waters, and hewed them out cisterns, broken cisterns, that can hold no water."

Here is a picture of this world. Men have turned away from Christ, the Fountain of living water, and have turned to the fading fountains of this world.

Many times people think they have discovered something which will bring them peace and happiness, but after awhile it vanishes. Such is not true of the water of life. It is always increasing, never diminishing.

The world cannot give abundant life; it can only give a momentary thrill. But in Jesus there is life abundant.

Some years ago an aunt and uncle of mine moved out of their little farm into the city. Back on the farm my aunt had carried water from a well almost a quarter of a mile. It was for drinking, for bathing and for washing clothes. That job never seemed to end. When they moved to the city, she would walk into the kitchen, turn on the faucet, let the water run into the sink, look at it and marvel at its abundance.

Oh, that God might make us tired of trying to carry water from the world's vile springs! Oh, that we might cease from our trying and learn to rest on Him, to find in Him abundance of peace, joy and rest!

Come to Jesus! Here is abundance for your life.

Some people seem to increase in vision and vigor as they grow older. This is certainly because of contact with the fountain of life in Christ.

Someone has pointed out that there is a simple five-point test by which any layman can detect the first signs of growing old in himself:

1. Do you find it more difficult to remember events of the past twenty-four hours (which is technically known as immediate recall)?

2. Do you require more time to execute physical and mental tasks?

3. Do you tend to resist new ideas?

4. Do you see fewer goals ahead worth striving for than you once did?

5. Do you spend more and more time dwelling on the past?

If to all of these five questions your answer is yes, then it is a fair sign that you are probably growing old.

However, let it be said that men and women who keep their fervent fresh touch with Jesus have increasing vision and increasing spiritual vigor as they march down the highway of life. Around us we see many who are advanced in years but eternally young in spirit. They are happy, rejoicing and courageous.

Someone has said that the Devil has no happy, old people. Thank God, the Lord has many happy, old people! They drink not from the world's fountains but of the water of life, and from them flow rivers of living waters.

III. THE WATER THAT CHRIST GIVES IS LIFE-GIVING, NOT LIFE-DESTROYING

The fountains of this world destroy men. They damn souls and wreck usefulness. Think of some of these fountains.

First, the fountain of self. See the multitudes who worship self. Self is the center of all their thinking. Others are forgotten. Selfish ambitions and desires guide the life. Self is pampered and coddled instead of disciplined.

Those who drink from the fountain of self need to read from the Word of God and learn the truth of dying to self.

"Likewise reckon ye also yourselves to be dead indeed unto sin, but alive unto God through Jesus Christ our Lord."—Rom. 6:11.

Paul said,

"I am crucified with Christ: nevertheless I live; yet not I, but Christ liveth in me: and the life which I now live in the flesh I live by the faith of the Son of God, who loved me, and gave himself for me."—Gal. 2:20.

The Christian life is the out-living of the in-living Christ. The fountain of self will destroy, if not the soul, the usefulness of the individual.

Second, the fountain of pleasure. This fountain is gushing forth from every quarter of the sinful world. But it gives no satisfaction and leads to death. Paul said, "But she that liveth in pleasure is dead while she liveth" (I Tim. 5:6). The thousands drinking at the fountain of pleasure—they are dead while they live.

This fountain never satisfies. The more one drinks, the more one wants. Still there is no satisfaction. There is always a hungering and a thirsting.

Demas wanted to drink from this fountain when he left the apostle. "Demas hath forsaken me, having loved this present world, and is departed unto Thessalonica."

Third, the fountain of wealth. See the mad rush to get money. Notice what men will do in order to gain wealth. See how they sacrifice home, family, reputation and hope of Heaven.

They ignore God, ridicule the churches, despise the way of salvation, worship money and drink from the fountain of wealth.

The parable of the rich fool should be sufficient for all such people. This man laid up much goods. He ignored God and worshiped himself and his success. He talked to his soul: "Soul, thou hast much goods laid up for many years; take thine ease, eat, drink, and be merry." Ah, but wait a minute! God said, "Thou fool, this night thy soul shall be required of thee: then whose shall those things be, which thou hast provided?"

Jesus gave the application of the parable when He said, "So is he that layeth up treasure for himself, and is not rich toward God." In plain words, a man is a fool to worship money and think that the fountain of wealth will bring peace and joy. He is a fool who will die and leave all he has. He is poverty-stricken spiritually.

There seems to surge within the souls of men a desire for power—power to rule, power to subject others to themselves.

Nebuchadnezzar drank from this fountain until God brought him down to his knees and made him eat grass like the oxen. Then he opened his eyes and saw his foolish mistake.

Alexander the Great drank from the fountain of power. He died a miserable, disappointed young man.

Napoleon drank from the fountain of power. He wanted to rule the whole world. His success lasted but for awhile; then came failure and loss. The fountain of power destroyed him instead of bringing him life.

Hitler drank from the fountain of power. His perverted nature came to rejoice only when others were being crushed. The fountain of power gave him the germs of death, which led to his own destruction.

Stalin drank from the fountain of power. His fiendish, atheistic mind seemed to reach out after only one thing—the control of others. But Stalin is gone; yea, all who drink from the fountain of power come to destruction.

I repeat: the fountains of this world destroy. It is only in Christ that men have life. Christ gives the water of eternal youth.

It is for this reason that in this church we are continually exhorting men, women and young people to come to Christ. It is in Him that we live, move and have our being. It is in Christ that souls are saved. It is in Christ that men have the abundant life.

The tragedy is, many are seeking to find life and satisfaction outside of Christ, only to discover their mistake too late. Life is gone. Death knocks on the door; then it is all over.

A present-day preacher gave a radio message on "If I Should Die Before I Live." He was changing the third line of the familiar child's prayer. Instead of saying, "If I should die before I wake," he made it read, "If I should die before I live." The import of his sermon was that merely to exist like an animal and never to live like an eternal soul is tragic.

One of our great magazines carried a soul-moving story of the war. The writer was a soldier. He recounted the experiences of his outfit and gave a graphic description of one of his fellow soldiers, a low character. He had a vile tongue, mouthing the most blood-curdling profanities and boasting of the vilest, unclean escapades.

Whenever he was on leave, this soldier became drunk and frequented the lowest dives. He gambled and cursed, drank and caroused. Finally he died in one of his drunken brawls.

The author of the article, commenting on his death, wrote this striking, sobering sentence: **"I am not sorry he died. I am sorry he never began to live."**

What a tragedy that many die before they live, die before they accomplish anything for God, die before they win a soul to Christ, die before they realize any worthwhile ambition, die before they know the meaning of fellowship with Christ and walking with God!

Christ is the One who makes life worthwhile. He gives us vision, fills us with peace and sends us forth with power.

Therefore, the invitation is: Come to Christ. Take of the water of life freely. May I suggest also, though it should not be necessary to say this, stay with Christ. In His presence is fullness of joy.

A Fortune to Share

"So is he that layeth up treasure for himself, and is not rich toward God."—Luke 12:21.

"For there is no difference between the Jew and the Greek: for the same Lord over all is rich unto all that call upon him."—Rom. 10:12.

I. BELIEVE IT

No one debates the fact that our God is the owner of all. The "cattle upon a thousand hills" belong to Him. The silver and the gold are His.

We who have been saved by the Lord Jesus are sons of God: "But as many as received him, to them gave he power to become the sons of God, even to them that believe on his name" (John 1:12).

The riches of God belong to us. All spiritual blessings are ours, and one day we shall receive full possession of this whole earth.

We have life in Christ: "He that believeth on the Son hath everlasting life." Jesus is the life, and when we believe in Him we receive eternal life from Him.

We have peace in Christ. The Saviour said, "Peace I leave with you, my peace I give unto you: not as the world giveth, give I unto you. Let not your heart be troubled, neither let it be afraid" (John 14:27).

We have His presence with us: "Lo, I am with you alway, even unto the end of the world" (Matt. 28:20).

We have the Holy Spirit indwelling us. The promise of our Lord was to send the Holy Spirit to abide with us and to guide us into all truth.

We have the eternal promises of God, promises that can never fail. The Word tells us that God cannot lie.

The newspapers gave an account of a poor farmer who gave a palmist nine thousand dollars. He thought that his money would be doubled in some miraculous way, but he learned the shrewdness of a crook. His money was gone, and the one who stole it had disappeared.

Man promises and fails, but God promises and keeps His word.

In short, my friends, we have a fortune to share.

Some years ago a star salesman made a fortune and began publicizing his good luck in a book called *A Fortune to Share*.

I wish I could get every Christian to see the truth of this statement: We have a fortune to share. Perhaps I can emphasize it by these words: Be constantly reminding yourself of all that God has done for you. The world of bitterness and doubt steals the calm assurance that we have a fortune.

The Apostle Peter might have thought, *Is it true that I was once a wicked fisherman, profane and hardhearted, but Christ saved me? Yes, it is true. I have a fortune to share.*

The Apostle Paul might have thought, *Is it true that I was once a wicked church man, a Pharisee, and felt that I was right and all others wrong? Is it true that I have a fortune and that this fortune has been given to me to share with others?* Yes, Paul had a fortune to share.

It was the Apostle Paul who said, "This is a faithful saying and worthy of all acceptation, that Christ Jesus came into the world to save sinners, of whom I am chief."

Don't forget what God has done for you. Believe, rejoice and tell others!

Two lads returning from school one early spring day stopped to play beside a stream. The spring thaw had begun, and the water was high. One of the boys accidentally fell into the stream and was swept down by the swift, powerful current. The other lad ran along the bank until he came to a place where the stream flowed beneath an old fence. He crawled out on it and, as his pal came down the stream, grabbed him. With some difficulty he managed to pull him out.

The boy who so nearly lost his life had an experience that he could

not forget, and he never ceased to speak of his rescue and the one
who had saved him.

We, the redeemed of God, must never cease to speak of our Lord
who came down from Heaven's glory to save us. The psalmist exhorts us, "Let the redeemed of the Lord say so." If you have felt the
power of His saving grace and love, then tell others. How tragic to
keep silent when souls are in peril!

Yes, you have a fortune to share! Believe it!

II. REJOICE IN IT

The Apostle Paul was forever talking about rejoicing in the Lord.
In the little book of Philippians, the word *joy* appears many times.
There was such happiness on the part of the apostle that he could
never get away from all that God had done for him.

I am sure that Paul agreed with the one who said that happiness
is not in ourselves but is in God. There are indeed by-streams of happiness, such as affection for others and from others, doing good to
others, doing creative work, entertaining hope for the future, sitting in the sunlight of pleasant memories of the past; but these are
only by-springs. The real fountain and source of happiness is a state
of life and soul that is right with God and, therefore, right with man.

We who are saved have a fortune in Jesus Christ. Let us rejoice
in it. Let us give thanks daily for the unspeakable gift of salvation,
just as Paul did.

Reading the letters of the Apostle Paul, we find that prisons
couldn't dull his joy. Hardships couldn't make him turn away from
God. Opposition couldn't keep him from praising his Saviour. Ill
health—and he must have had much of it—couldn't close his mouth
and keep him from shouting praise to God.

If Paul could rejoice in his great salvation, then surely we can.

Children rejoice over small gifts. Then why should we not rejoice
over our great gift, the gift of everlasting life?

A poor man of the street may rejoice over a little gift of money.
Why should we not rejoice in the abundance which is given us by
the Lord?

Here is a drunkard: once he knew the awful ravages of sin and drink, but now he rejoices that he has been saved from sin and made sober and upright in the Lord. Here is a thief: once he was bound by the sin of thievery; then Jesus came in and saved his soul. He rejoices in the Lord.

If most of you could have placed in your hands a fortune of this world's goods, it is likely you would rejoice. But the chances are, your joy would soon vanish because it would not be founded in that which gives abiding joy.

In a few days it will be my privilege to speak in the famous Mel Trotter Mission in Grand Rapids, Michigan. A number of years ago I heard Mel Trotter preach in the First Presbyterian Church in Nashville, Tennessee. I heard only one of his messages, but in that sermon was so much joy and happiness, so much of the Spirit of Christ that I never forgot it.

Mel Trotter had been a drunken thief. He had taken the shoes from the body of his dead baby and sold them to buy liquor. But Jesus Christ saved Mel Trotter. He began going everywhere and telling the story of his redemption. There was a joy, a vibrancy, a life in Mel Trotter which people could never forget. He rejoiced in his salvation.

III. SHARE IT

The whole Bible shouts the doctrine of sharing what we have. This is the spirit of our Saviour. This was the spirit of Paul. This was the spirit of Peter. And this has been the spirit of every truly born again man and woman.

There is something wrong with you if you don't care to share your salvation, if you're not concerned about others and their needs.

Now, let me give it to you in three statements:

First, let us see the need of others. Men and women without Jesus Christ are lost and undone, without God and without hope. "The soul that sinneth, it shall die." All are sinners, and all are under the sentence of death.

Nicodemus was a good man, a ruler of the people, a keeper of the law; but he was lost nevertheless. He had to be born again to be saved.

Zacchaeus was perhaps a good man in many respects, but unsaved. He had to be born again.

The poor lame man, healed by Peter and John, had need of salvation and healing, and received it in the name of Jesus Christ.

Even when others do not see their need, we must not fail to see it. We must recognize that men and women without Christ are lost. Their eternal souls are bound for Hell. They may be blinded by the world and deafened by the world's clamor, but they must see that Christ is the Saviour. We must see their need of Him.

Second, we must have compassion and concern for others. Jesus looked upon the multitudes and wept over them. When we look upon lost people, are we stirred in our hearts to do something for them? I can see that they are unsaved, but am I moved by their condition?

In some miraculous way, may we have our eyes opened to see the multitudes. God grant that we might see people as lost or saved—see them only in this way. May they not be divided by their position in life but by their acceptance or rejection of Jesus Christ.

Most of us were stirred when we read in the morning paper the account of the missionary fliers lost in South America. One doubtless lost his life. Some were sent out by Missionary Aviation Fellowship, which we have had a part in aiding.

First, let us not forget that it was missionary concern for others which sent them into the field. They had compassion for others. So must we. If these five men who are lost in South America were members of your families, it would not be hard to get you to respond to an all-night prayer meeting in their behalf. Thank God, all of these men are devout Christians, but around the world there are many without our Saviour. May we have concern and compassion for others.

Third, may we share what we have. May we give to others, tell others of Christ, and witness to others regarding our Saviour. Call this work whatever you will, but be sure you do it. We have a fortune to share. God has been good to us. Now we must show others that we have something that they need. Don't be selfish, but go with the Gospel.

There was a day when John the Baptist stood with two of his disciples and, looking upon Jesus as He walked, said, "Behold the

Lamb of God"! The two disciples who were in the company of John left him and followed Jesus. Jesus turned and saw them following and said, "What seek ye?" And they said unto Him, "Rabbi, where dwellest thou?" Jesus said, "Come and see." They came and saw where He dwelt and abode with Him that day, for it was about the tenth hour.

"One of the two which heard John speak, and followed him, was Andrew." Andrew must have thought, *I have something good. I have been saved. Christ is my Saviour. I know something that others need to know, and I must do something about it.*

The next words in our Bible are these: "He first findeth his own brother Simon, and saith unto him, We have found the Messias, which is, being interpreted, the Christ. And he brought him to Jesus."

That job is given to every one of us. The task must be done. We must share our joy, our fortune with others. We must not fail to tell others of our blessed Saviour!

The Mad Race

"But seek ye first the kingdom of God, and his righteousness; and all these things shall be added unto you."—Matt. 6:33.

"I therefore so run, not as uncertainly; so fight I, not as one that beateth the air: But I keep under my body, and bring it into subjection: lest that by any means, when I have preached to others, I myself should be a castaway."—I Cor. 9:26,27.

The world is in a mad race—a race for things which vanish like snow under a July sun.

The world is in a race to make money. Every paper, magazine, radio announcement—all are telling us how to make money, how to get ahead. People are being taught to love money.

But listen to I Timothy 6:10: "For the love of money is the root of all evil: which while some coveted after, they have erred from the faith, and pierced themselves through with many sorrows."

To Timothy, Paul gave an urgent appeal to turn away from money and follow after "righteousness, godliness, faith, love, patience, and meekness."

Many are in a race for fame. They desire to see their names in the limelight. They want to know that they have achieved a place in society and in the leadership of men.

Still others are racing for popularity. First place is their desire. They seek not the things of God but the things of this world.

Still others are in a mad race for pleasure. This takes in literally millions of people. It doubtless took in Demas in the days of the Apostle Paul, for Paul said of him, "For Demas hath forsaken me, having loved this present world, and is departed unto Thessalonica..." (II Tim. 4:10).

A mad race—yet how swiftly these things disappear. The famous people of a few years ago are mere names in history books. The Alexanders and the Napoleons find their places along with the Hitlers and the Mussolinis, and all are forgotten.

Yet man is driving himself forward in an effort to gain the things of this world. He is in a mad race, caring not whom he hurts on the way. He is interested only in reaching the goal for himself.

As I studied for this message, I turned to a book which I had read carefully some years ago. I came to page 100 in this book, and on the margin I had written down the name of a friend of mine and his telephone number. As I looked at his name and visioned what had happened to him, I thought how vividly this illustrates the entire message.

Here was a man who sought fame, who desired the world's acclaim. After awhile he turned to seeking fame and the things of the flesh. He was in a mad race for the things of this world.

But after awhile he lost everything. Though still a young man, all is gone. His life is empty. His talents are wasted.

Now we come to this question: What should we desire? What things should be first in our lives?

We should desire to

I. KNOW CHRIST AS PERSONAL SAVIOUR

Without question, this is the greatest thing of all—to be able to say with the Apostle Paul, "For I know whom I have believed, and am persuaded that he is able to keep that which I have committed unto him against that day" (II Tim. 1:12).

It is a sweet and reassuring thought when we can know that we are saved. There need be no doubt about this matter. The child of God can be definitely assured by this infallible Word that he is God's child. It is not a matter of boasting but a simple matter of knowing.

Salvation means Heaven. When one is saved, he is ready for that beautiful home which our Lord has gone to prepare for him. Oh, my friend, believe His promise and rest in His love.

Am I speaking to some sinner who has never accepted Jesus Christ?

Then I want you to know there is nothing more important than knowing that Christ is your Saviour.

One preacher expressed it like this:

> Never mind about the irreconcilability of free will and fore-ordination. Get ready for eternity.
>
> Never mind about who wrote the Pentateuch. Get ready for eternity.
>
> Never mind about the things of the Bible you can't understand. Get ready for eternity.
>
> Never mind about the inconsistencies of some church members you know. Get ready for eternity.
>
> Before the sun shall have rounded out another year, you may be there. You have 365 days to live and possibly not so many. You are going down to the grave. The pale horse with his rider is on his way. You are standing on the border of eternity. You are hurrying to judgment and to the recompense of reward.
>
> Why should the pleasures, the honors, the business of this world hold you so fast that you have no time or disposition to think of the hereafter? Why should you be forever looking in your safety deposit boxes and forget about what you have in your breast?
>
> When Lord Rosebery, the brilliant, the careless young Parliamentarian, was dying, William E. Gladstone, the massive-minded statesman of England, stood by his bedside; and three times he said, "Lord Rosebery, take care of your soul."

There is nothing more important that I could press upon you than your own soul's need. Do you know Christ as Saviour? If you do not, then repent of your sin and believe in Jesus Christ at this very moment.

Certainly one thing every person should desire is to know Christ as personal Saviour.

We should desire to

II. DO HIS WILL

When Paul met Jesus on the road to Damascus, or maybe I should say, when the Lord met Paul, we find Paul trembling and astonished, saying, "Lord, what wilt thou have me to do?"

There are those who may argue about the matter, but they do foolishly and without reason. This is a self-evident fact: Paul had come face to face with the Lord and had made a definite surrender of himself to Christ. He was ready now for God to have His way.

As a child of God, is there anything more desirable for you than to say, "Lord, Thy will be done"?

Is there anything that could bring greater pleasure, joy and contentment to you than to commit yourself completely to the will of God?

Here is a matter which is above fame, fortune, popularity and success. Here is a matter which is above health and physical well-being. Nothing is more important for you than the will of God.

Are you afraid of His will? fearful that He might ask you to do something which is hard and not according to the flesh? Let me assure you that the will of God will always bring the greatest contentment when you surrender to it.

Young man, if God wants you in His ministry, be quick to say, "Lord, I am ready to do Thy will." Do not give excuses and seek to find a way out, but quickly agree with the Lord and enter into His work.

Young lady, if God has called you into some service of our Christ, then, without hesitation, give yourself to the Lord and do His will.

This mad racing humanity is so unconcerned about the will of God. But I hasten to say that there is nothing more important for you as a child of God than His will for your life.

What should we desire?

III. TO REACH OTHERS FOR CHRIST

Let me hit a hard blow at selfishness! Back of 99% of our failures in soul winning is selfishness. The reason more of us are not moving out into the field and winning precious souls is selfishness. We want to see people saved, we like to see them respond to the invitations; but we are too selfish, too consumed with our own purposes and desires to do the will of God. And let it be remembered that reaching others for Christ is God's will for you.

Do you care for others? Are you concerned about their salvation? Is there a love burning in your soul which demands that you reach people for Christ? If so, then you cannot stay back; but you must do the task that God has given you to do.

In Dallas, Texas, is located the Buckner Orphans' Home. In the early years of the orphanage, the superintendent, Dr. Buckner, would be away for weeks, raising funds for the institution. When it was

announced to the children that Daddy Buckner was to return at some
definite time, the home was buzzing with excitement. All hearts were
aflutter with anticipation. The children would put on their best
clothes, and many would gather beautiful bouquets for the returning superintendent.

In those days there lived in the orphanage a little half-witted
girl. She didn't know the difference between sticks, weeds and flowers.
When Dr. Buckner would return, scores of little children would press
upon him, trying to be the first to place kisses of affection upon his
cheeks and to show their love in the presentation of their bouquets.

As the kindhearted man stood in their midst, it could be clearly
seen that he was looking for someone, yes, some special one. There
she stood out on the fringe of that crowd of children, abashed and
fearful, holding in her little hands her bouquet of sticks and weeds.

Dr. Buckner, pushing aside the others for the moment, would
go to the small, half-witted girl, take her in his strong arms and speak
comforting, tender words to her little heart.

Oh, could it be that in this great task of winning souls, we have
failed to love others as we should love them? that we do not have
the compassion for their souls that we should have? May God speak
to us. May we begin to show compassion and love for a lost world.

What are the names of the men we remember? They are the men
who first sought God; second, they lived to please Him; third, they
served God by reaching after others.

Those who are thinking straight about that which is before us
tonight have no desire to be members of the mad race, no desire to
seek fame, fortune, popularity, success—those things which quickly
pass away. We wholly want to do the will of God.

Remember back in the ancient days there was no water for the
army until ditches were dug (II Kings 3:16,17). There was no oil until the vessels were gathered (II Kings 4:3). There was no healing
until the leper had dipped seven times (II Kings 5:10). There was
no harvest until the ground had been broken up (Hosea 10:12). There
was no vision without obedience (John 9:7).

God wants to pour out blessings on us, but He waits for our willingness and readiness to receive those blessings.

The Covered Radio

"And he spake a parable unto them to this end, that men ought always to pray, and not to faint."—Luke 18:1.

Radio has always had a special fascination for me. Since the day when I listened to my first handmade radio set, I have been conscious that radio is from the hand of God.

First, it is God's plan for man to have the radio. He made the earth and the air surrounding it in such a way that sound waves could be carried thousands of miles and man could hear in distant places.

Second, I am aware that radio has been used to get the Gospel out around the world. Today some stations spend twenty-four hours daily broadcasting the message of our Saviour.

I could add other reasons why radio has a special attraction for me, but these will suffice.

However, in spite of my love for radio and my appreciation for its God-given worth, I have allowed a very simple thing to crowd it out. Through the years it has always been the same. The radio I listen to the most will be the one at the side of my bed. This radio often becomes covered with books and papers. The controls cannot be reached. The radio is silent. Its mechanism is in perfect working order, but it is silent. The radio with its ability to bring messages and music into the home is not heard because it is covered and almost hidden by other things.

The radio, covered and silent, illustrates prayer crowded out. It is ours to turn on the controls and to talk to God, but the controls are too often covered by all the extraneous devices of this world. Prayer is crowded out.

Some of the things which crowd out prayer and its effectiveness may be good, but they are used of Satan to keep us from a most important work.

Now consider three simple points:

I. PRAYER IS COMMANDED BY THE WORD

"Seek ye the Lord while he may be found, call ye upon him while he is near."—Isa. 55:6.

"Ask, and it shall be given you; seek, and ye shall find; knock, and it shall be opened unto you: For every one that asketh receiveth; and he that seeketh findeth; and to him that knocketh it shall be opened."— Matt. 7:7,8.

"Watch and pray, that ye enter not into temptation: the spirit indeed is willing, but the flesh is weak."—Matt. 26:41.

"Watch ye therefore, and pray always, that ye may be accounted worthy to escape all these things that shall come to pass, and to stand before the Son of man."—Luke 21:36.

"Praying always with all prayer and supplication in the Spirit, and watching thereunto with all perseverance and supplication for all saints."—Eph. 6:18.

"Be careful for nothing; but in every thing by prayer and supplication with thanksgiving let your requests be made known unto God. And the peace of God, which passeth all understanding, shall keep your hearts and minds through Christ Jesus."—Phil. 4:6,7.

"Continue in prayer, and watch in the same with thanksgiving."— Col. 4:2.

"Pray without ceasing."—I Thess. 5:17.

"I exhort therefore, that, first of all, supplications, prayers, intercessions, and giving of thanks, be made for all men."—I Tim. 2:1.

Yes, the Bible commands us to pray. We are told to "ask," "seek," "knock." We are told to pray about everything, and then "the peace of God which passeth all understanding shall keep your hearts and minds through Christ Jesus.''

Prayer was commanded by the Lord, and prayer was illustrated by our Saviour. Jesus, the Son of God, was a man of prayer. He who prayed in times of crisis, He who prayed in the early morning hours, He who prayed all night long, commands us to pray.

There is nothing greater any one of us can do than spend time in earnest prayer. Yet perhaps this one thing we fail to do more than all else.

The power of prayer has been illustrated by our modern guns. Here is a great modern cannon, one of those big guns about which we have heard so much. The long and graceful barrel of the gun is pointing toward the foe.

But there is nothing in that barrel. Birds could nest in it. Here is the wheel that elevates and lowers the gun. But there is nothing in that wheel itself which would strike against the enemy. Here is the range finder, a delicate and beautiful instrument; here is the shell or cartridge with the power back of it, ready to be hurled against the foe. But there is nothing in that shell itself which can injure the enemy.

Back of the gun is the gunner, ready to do his work, with strong mind and trained hands. But in himself there is nothing, no power that can hurt the enemy. It is only when the spark of fire is applied to the powder that the great cannon, with its intricate mechanism, its death-dealing shell, its trained gunners, becomes an instrument of power and destruction.

We can talk about prayer, study prayer and preach about it; but nothing happens unless we pray and obey the commands of the Word.

II. PRAYER IS CROWDED OUT BY THE WORLD

When we study why people do not pray, we arrive at a number of conclusions.

First, people do not turn away from the place of prayer because they hate God. It is not because God has been unfair to them.

Second, it is not because of doubts regarding the efficacy of prayer that men fail to pray. We know that God answers prayer. The greatest things that have ever happened to us have come because we prayed.

Third, it is not disappointment because of past failures that keeps us from prayer. We have failed many times. Our hearts have been broken by our failures. These are not the things which keep us from prayer.

Then why don't we pray? Let's see if there is some definite word we can say regarding prayer.

First, we do not pray because we have absurd ideas of our own ability. We imagine that we can do the job ourselves, so why bother God? I heard a preacher make the statement that he thought it was wrong to bother God about small things. He advocated that a person simply do his best and not bother God about these minute matters of life.

I thought his was a good statement—as a matter of fact, I repeated it a few times—then I saw the folly of it. I am limited. I can do only so much. God's power is unlimited. He can do all things. My prayers must be about all matters, not simply some great things, but everything, great and small.

Second, we do not pray because we are too busy. The affairs of life crowd in. Our world becomes more and more demanding of our time. Our busy lives in business, in pleasure, in church activities—all of these things keep us from God and from prayer. Some of the things which hinder us may seem worthwhile from the human standpoint, but in God's sight, they are not important. Prayer should ever be first.

Third, we do not pray because we fail to see the greatness of prayer. There is nothing greater you can do than call upon God's name. Here you are, a poor, finite, limited person. Here is God with infinite power. Prayer puts you in touch with God.

Realize the greatness of prayer, your need for spending more time in talking with God.

Yesterday a man talked with me about the meaning of prayer. He told of spending seven months in a hospital. They despaired of his life. Finally on New Year's Eve, the doctors gave a verdict that he would have to have a certain operation and the outcome of it would be very doubtful.

This man was a pastor of a church. That night, New Year's Eve, some 800 of his people met together and prayed that God would heal their pastor and bring him back to them.

The preacher said that in a most miraculous way, about five minutes before twelve, the condition which had been troubling him for a long time began to straighten out. When the doctors came to see him the next time, they stated that a very strange thing had happened. There was now no need for the operation which they had planned.

O friends, may we see the greatness of prayer! Sometimes illness may be for a special divine purpose. Again, God may see fit to give healing when it is for His glory.

III. PRAYER IS COMMENDED BY MEN OF GOD

We have discussed, first, that prayer is commanded by the Word; second, prayer is crowded out by the world; and now may we consider that prayer is commended by men of God.

Abraham was a man of prayer. He was called the friend of God, and I believe that this designation was because of his fervent looking to the Lord in prayer. The picture of Abraham, the intercessor, is given in Genesis 18:23-33. Abraham began pleading with the Lord to spare Sodom if only a few righteous could be found.

Abraham was a man of prayer.

King David was a man of prayer. You have simply to open your Bible to the Psalms and see the prayers of David. He constantly called upon the name of the Lord. Hear him as he says:

"Unto thee will I cry, O Lord my rock; be not silent to me. . . . Hear the voice of my supplications, when I cry unto thee, when I lift up my hands toward thy holy oracle."—Ps. 28:1,2.

Almost every Psalm is a cry unto the Lord.

Elijah was a man of prayer. See the noble prophet as he stood at Mt. Carmel and faced the worshipers of Baal. See him as he prayed and fire fell from Heaven, consumed the burnt sacrifice, the wood, stones, dust and licked up the water in the trench.

Elijah was a man of prayer.

Daniel was a man of prayer. Often we find that Daniel looked to the Lord and sought the face of God in prayer.

The Apostle Peter was a man of prayer. The greatness of his life, from Pentecost on, was built on the foundation of faith in God and fervent prayer. His whole life as a minister of the Gospel was built around the altar of prayer. When he was cast into prison, he prayed, and the people prayed for him.

The Apostle Paul was a man of prayer. In every situation, when opposition came against him, when unbelievers sought to defeat him, he cried unto the Lord, and God heard and answered his prayers.

Now, prayer is commended by men of God. Commended why? because it works. Commended why? because it brings to pass that which is desired.

David Brainerd prayed, and revival came among the American Indians. He stands today as one who found access to God in prayer and who accomplished great things through this heavenly medium.

George Mueller was a man of prayer. For over sixty years 2,000 orphans were fed three times daily because this man prayed.

R. A. Torrey, the evangelist, was a man of prayer.

I do not have time to enumerate the names of men who commend prayer and tell us that prayer is the only way to be victorious with our Lord.

Will you say tonight, "I want to be a person of prayer; I want God to take over in my life and direct me day by day"? Will you let prayer, real prayer, fervent prayer, be a definite part of your life? Will you set aside certain times each day for prayer? Will you make it a habit to go to the Lord in definite prayer at all seasons? Will you pray regarding every problem that may come up? Will you seek the face of our Lord at all times?

Be careful that prayer has its essential place in your life, and do not let the world crowd it out.

> If radio's slim fingers can pluck a melody from night,
> And toss it over a continent or sea;
> If the petalled white notes of a violin
> Are blown across a mountain or a city's din;
> If songs like crimson roses are culled from thin blue air,
> Why should mortals wonder if God hears prayer?

10 Dragnet

"*Again, the kingdom of heaven is like unto a net, that was cast into the sea, and gathered of every kind.*"—Matt. 13:47.

Some Bible truths come to new Christians with a distinct shock.

First, it is a surprise to them to discover that the whole world will not be saved. In spite of all our efforts, the entire world will not turn to Christ. We may evangelize, but we will not Christianize. The postmillennial concept, which dwelt on the theory that the whole world would be won to Christ and that man would usher in the kingdom, is not true. The Word says that, when we come to the end of the age, the angel shall come forth and sever the wicked from among the just.

So it is a shock to Christians to discover that the Word does not teach that everyone will be saved or that man will succeed in ushering in the kingdom.

Second, it is a shock to new Christians to find that all church members are not saved. When a man has just found Christ as Saviour, he enters his new life with devotion and dedication. In the early stages of his new-found salvation, he is prepared to give all to Christ. He usually believes that all church members are saved, dedicated, unselfish and wholesome. It is alarming to him to discover that many professing church members do not know Christ and that still others who profess to know Him are far from dedication and surrender.

It is a good day for the child of God when he discovers the three classifications of people as given in the Word of God.

First, there is the natural man, who is still in the flesh and un-saved. According to I Corinthians 2:14, "But the natural man receiveth not the things of the Spirit of God: for they are foolishness unto him: neither can he know them, because they are spiritually discerned."

Second, there is the carnal man, designated by Paul as a "babe in Christ." The carnal person is guilty of envy, strife and divisions. Though saved, he is walking according to the flesh and not fully after the Spirit.

Third, there is the spiritual man, who is consecrated to the will of God and ready to serve God.

Happy is he who comes to the place where he says, "I am deter-mined to be classified as a spiritual one." He then turns from the worldly walk. He refuses to behave after the flesh. He walks as one directed by the Spirit of God.

Which are you today? natural? carnal? spiritual? The natural man needs Christ as Saviour. The carnal man needs to face himself and his need and look to the Lord instead of to man and to self. The spiritual man needs to continue to grow in grace and in knowledge.

Many of our church difficulties come because in our membership we have the natural and the carnal. The natural man does not even understand spiritual things, and therefore he will cause trouble. The carnal man is walking as men and cannot contribute to the spiritual program of the church. He will always vote according to the flesh. He is a babe in Christ, easily offended, disturbed by small things, quite often getting upset.

When we have revivals, Christians may get revived; but revival never touches a lost man. His need is salvation. I feel that, when we are disturbed because the revival made such little change in peo-ple, we have expected to revive a dead corpse. Christians can be revived; lost church members need salvation.

Now, I want us to look at the parable of the dragnet.

"Again, the kingdom of heaven is like unto a net, that was cast into the sea, and gathered of every kind:

"Which, when it was full, they drew to shore, and sat down, and

gathered the good into vessels, but cast the bad away.

"So shall it be at the end of the world: the angels shall come forth, and sever the wicked from among the just,

"And shall cast them into the furnace of fire: there shall be wailing and gnashing of teeth."—Matt. 13:47-50.

There are three three-letter words that I want to use to summarize the lesson.

I. THE SEA

"The kingdom of heaven is like unto a net, that was cast into the sea...." The sea here represents the world, or the great mass of humanity.

Habakkuk said that God "makest men as the fishes of the sea, as the creeping things, that have no ruler over them" (1:14).

Humanity is like the sea. First, the sea is troubled by adverse winds. Humanity is troubled. Storms rage and beat in upon sinful man. "There is no rest, saith my God, to the wicked."

Second, the sea is always changing. It is never quite the same. So it is with man. He is tossed about by every wind of doctrine. He is constantly changing his opinions. That which was thought scientifically true twenty-five years ago has been proven untrue today. Nothing is steadfast as far as man is concerned.

Third, the sea is full of death and destruction. So it is with humanity. Death stalks every man. "It is appointed unto men once to die, but after this the judgment."

Our need is to see our world and its great need. Two-thirds of the world is yet without Jesus Christ. Men are under bondage to sin and Satan, bound by superstition, darkness and doubt.

Though we may be disgusted at times with man's foolishness, let us not lose our compassion for a lost world.

II. THE NET

"The kingdom of heaven is like unto a net." This is referring, not to a small hand net, but to a large net that is cast into the sea to gather in great quantities of fish.

The preaching of the gospel message is the net. The giving out of the Word of God through every quarter of the earth is the casting forth of the net.

At the very climax of the gospel message is God's invitation for men to come to Him. This invitation is universal and extended to all men.

Second, we are the fishermen. We are to cast the net. When Jesus called Simon and Andrew at the Sea of Galilee, they were casting a net into the sea; for they were fishermen. When Jesus said to them, "Come ye after me, and I will make you to become fishers of men," they straightway left everything and followed Him.

The same invitation is given to us. We are invited to follow Him and to be fishers of men.

When a person is first saved, one of the evidences of salvation is a desire to cast the net and to win someone else to Jesus. Too soon this desire seems to cool and fade. Fear enters the hearts of some. They are afraid to cast the net, afraid of what man may say. Timidity makes them hold back instead of boldly launching out.

Some hesitate to cast the net because of their experiences. For example, they have seen some make professions of faith, then fade away. Because of this, they have said, "It is a worthless task." Don't be afraid of casting the net, for this is the command of our Lord, and it is ours to be faithful.

Let us not be afraid of gathering in the bad with the good. When the dragnet goes out, it brings in the bad fish as well as the good fish. It brings in worthless rubbish as well as that which is valuable.

Cast the net—give the Gospel—every day and in every place. Do not seek for the favorable time, but take advantage of the present moment.

Third, the net gathers of every kind. Though the net is intended for catching that which is good, it will gather in that which is bad.

We see a demonstration of this in the very work of our church. The Gospel is given from this pulpit faithfully Sunday after Sunday and Wednesday after Wednesday. Our people go out into the highways and hedges and give out the message of Christ. We have almost encompassed every portion of the city in the dragnet, which is preaching the gospel message. As a result of our efforts, many have been saved through faith in Christ; but many have been brought in who seem to know nothing of our Christ.

Let us not be disturbed by this, but be prayerful and earnest that we might help those who have come into our midst without knowing Christ in salvation. The same thing was true in the church in Corinth and in Philippi. In Philippi there were some in their midst whom Paul called "the enemies of the cross of Christ."

III. THE END

"So shall it be at the end of the world." This speaks of the consummation of the age.

There is coming a time when the net will be full. "Which, when it was full, they drew to shore, and sat down, and gathered the good into vessels, but cast the bad away."

The net is now filling. The message is going out. Many are being brought in. One day our Lord will come, and this age will be brought to a close.

At the end of this age there will be a separation. "The angels shall come forth, and sever the wicked from among the just."

There will be a separation at the coming of Christ for His own.

"I tell you, in that night there shall be two men in one bed; the one shall be taken, and the other shall be left. Two women shall be grinding together; the one shall be taken, and the other left."—Luke 17:34,35.

There will be further separation—when Christ comes in the revelation and the nations are gathered before Him.

Please note the Lord said, "The angels shall come forth, and sever the wicked from among the just." We cannot see what is in the net, so we must not judge others. The separation will be made by the angels of God.

Remember this: the good and the bad will not always be together. Today possessors and professors are mingled together, even in one local church; but there will come a time when they will be separated—hypocrites from true Christians.

Many have been deceived regarding the way of salvation, some by false teachers and by false churches. The way of salvation has been perverted, and men have been deceived into thinking they are saved. Others have been deceived by their own flesh, still others by their friends. Back of all deception is Satan, who desires the damnation of all men.

Be careful in your teaching. Let men know that salvation is by grace through faith in Jesus Christ. Emphasize again and again that salvation is not by works nor by baptism nor by church membership. Warn people of the poisonous doctrines which are being circulated around the world. Give them the pure gospel message of salvation through faith in Jesus Christ.

The time of separation is coming. Are you saved or lost? Will you be among the good gathered into the mansions of Glory, or will you be cast away with the bad?

Third, and last, notice the destiny. The dragnet gathered in the good and the bad. The good was brought into vessels, and the evil—the bad—was cast away. When Christ comes for His own, the saints will be caught up to meet Him in the air, and the unsaved will be left for the awful Tribulation suffering. The suffering of this period will be beyond all human description, but after that will come the suffering of Hell, which will go on forever and forever.

Do you know Christ as your Saviour? Do you possess eternal life? It is not enough that you are a church member; the question is, are you among the good or the bad, the saved or the lost? Though you may belong to a dozen churches, if you know not Christ, you will be separated from the saved and be lost forever.

Are you saved? Do you know that Christ is your personal Saviour? It is not a matter of "thinking so" or "hoping so"—but do you have the assurance that you belong to Him?

11 The Place of Memory in the Christian's Life

"Remember Lot's wife."—Luke 17:32.

Memory must have a strong place in the Christian's life. If we carelessly forget certain events or allow memory to dull them, we are going to suffer.

Remember your salvation. Never get away from the time when you accepted Jesus Christ as Saviour. Though it may have occurred in childhood, refresh your mind often regarding what Christ has done for you.

Remember your decisions for consecration. Those driving moments, when all else seemed of little value, your one decision was to give Christ your best. Keep this before you. Don't allow the passing of years to make you forget.

Remember your acceptance of God's plan of giving. You saw that this was right and honest. You understood that the tithe belonged to the Lord. You began tithing—have you continued? Strong words are given to those who turn aside. The Word of God calls them "robbers." "Will a man rob God? Yet ye have robbed me. But ye say, Wherein have we robbed thee? In tithes and offerings" (Mal. 3:8).

Remember your pledge for soul winning. With real intent of heart, you began to witness to others. What happened? You got too busy. The response was not as great as you had hoped for. You discontinued, or maybe you are still engaged in this momentous work. If so, pause and praise God for that which He has done for you and that which He will do for others if we witness to them.

Maybe I am speaking to some who need to be reminded of God's call. Have you been true to His call? Are you doing what God wants you to do? Happiness is in the place of His choosing.

Now let us turn to the text. Jesus said, "Remember Lot's wife." Why would our Saviour give this exhortation? Because of its importance. The Son of God wasted no words.

Lot turned away from Abraham and dwelled in Sodom. There came the day when God had to destroy Sodom because of her sin. He gave warning to Lot and his family. His sons-in-law laughed at him; but Lot took his wife and daughters and fled from the city.

The Lord told Lot and his family, "Look not behind thee." Lot escaped from the city and started out across the plains. Brimstone and fire rained down upon Sodom and Gomorrah while Lot and his wife and daughters were making their escape; but his wife looked back, and "she became a pillar of salt" (Gen. 19:26).

After this strange and unusual happening, we wonder that anyone would mention again the strange occurrence of Lot's wife; but in His message to the disciples on the subject of the second coming, our Lord said, "Remember Lot's wife."

Let us see what He had in mind for us.

Remember Lot's wife

I. BECAUSE THERE IS DANGER IN LOOKING BACK

There was sore danger for Lot's wife. She became a pillar of salt. There is danger when you look back.

First, the danger of lamenting over your physical and material losses. Lot's wife, doubtless, did this. She saw all of her finery going up in the smoke of Sodom. It was not easy for her to turn her back upon all that she had.

My wife and I were talking today about a couple I led to the Lord in Fairfield, Alabama. When the man first came to my door, he was pitiful looking. He was bitter of mind and of heart. He told me of the rich fortune that had been his for many years, then how when the Depression came, all of his goods were swept away in a moment's time.

Some years had gone by, and he was still worrying about those losses. I showed him that there was much more ahead of him. He and his wife accepted Christ as Saviour. Both became faithful members of the church. They didn't have much of this world's goods, but they had a glorious future.

I repeat: There is a danger in lamenting over your physical and material losses. Do not waste time weeping over the losses of yesterday. Set your face forward and move on for God.

Second, the danger of worrying about your mistakes. If some mistakes can be rectified, they need to be rectified. Some cannot be rectified; therefore, they must be forgotten. We must make things right with God and press forward. If our mistake is in the nature of sin, we can claim I John 1:9, confess it to the Lord, then redouble our efforts to serve God.

Third, the danger of losing sight of the grand events of the future. The greatest things are yet to come. The greatest days are yet ahead. Don't look back and feel that you have lost so much, either by age or by change of circumstances. There is danger in looking back! Press forward!

Remember Lot's wife

II. BECAUSE THE BEST IS AHEAD

She looked back. We must not do so.

Whatever you may have now, the best is ahead. The coming of our Saviour is the great truth of God upon which we must rest. He is coming! We will join with our loved ones. The day of turmoil, strife, envy, malice, jealousy and dissension will be over. The best is ahead! There will be a blessed reunion with all of our loved ones.

"For the Lord himself shall descend from heaven with a shout, with the voice of the archangel, and with the trump of God: and the dead in Christ shall rise first: Then we which are alive and remain shall be caught up together with them in the clouds, to meet the Lord in the air: and so shall we ever be with the Lord."—I Thess. 4:16, 17.

Yes, look ahead! A day of reunion is coming. The dead in Christ shall be raised, the living shall be changed, and together we shall meet our Lord in the air. Is it any wonder that the apostle puts down,

"Wherefore, comfort one another with these words"?

Again, the best is ahead because there is coming a day of freedom from besetting fears. So many of you are engrossed in various problems and difficulties. Fears beset you. You wonder if you are going to be able to go forward. Oh, my friend, don't look back! The best is ahead!

Remember Lot's wife

III. BECAUSE THERE IS A DIGNITY IN OBEDIENCE

God said, "Don't look back." But Lot's wife disobeyed God and looked back. The Word says, "To obey is better than sacrifice." Above all, God is asking for our obedience.

First, obey God whatever men may say. Man would discourage. Here is a man preparing for the ministry. Friends may say, "You are very foolish." Not so—he is very wise for obeying God.

Second, obey God despite circumstances. All things may be against you. There may be no money, no prospects of success; but do what God says, and He will see you through.

Third, obey God and rejoice in it. Give obedience with alacrity and joy. Don't be slow in obeying Him. He does not lead foolishly. Rejoice that you can obey the Heavenly Father.

Keep your mind set on doing His will whatever conditions may surround you.

During the Civil War, a messenger riding into the hometown of General Stonewall Jackson deposited a letter from the general in the hand of the pastor. An anxious crowd gathered on the church steps as the letter was opened, expecting some news of the war— news about Missionary Ridge or Lookout Mountain. But the letter read,

My dear Pastor:

I recalled today that my gift to foreign missions was due. Find it enclosed.

May the day soon come when this war is over. May the right side win that we may go back to our primary task of saving the souls of men.

This letter from the general shows that his heart was set upon the main business—that of winning souls.

Obey God because you are a child of the King.

Some African slaves were marching in chains toward the ship that would take them to the land of slavery. They were shuffling along discouraged, melancholy and with heads bowed toward the ground.

But one young man walked with a kingly bearing, with head thrown back and shoulders squared. One of the slave drivers asked, "Who is that man?" To this, another slave driver replied, "He is the son of an African king, and he cannot forget it."

While other men are shuffling along, discouraged, uncouth and unprincely, remember that you are a child of God and you should give your obedience to Him and to His service.

There is a solemn and beautiful dignity in obedience. God grant that all of you will say, "I want to obey my Saviour and do what He says at all times."

Obey Him because there will be an accounting day. We may not understand everything now, but one day it will be made clear.

There is the story of a certain woman who was visiting Heaven—a woman who had had considerable means on earth. As she passed a rather modest bungalow, she said somewhat lightly to Saint Peter, "And whose bungalow is this?"

He answered, "Yours, Madam."

Rather disappointed they walked on. She spied a large estate, a costly mansion, and asked, "And whose is this?"

Peter replied, "That estate belongs to Harry Smith."

"Strange," said she. "Harry Smith is the name of my chauffeur."

He said, "That's right. It is Harry Smith's. You see, Madam, in building a mansion up here in Heaven, we have only such materials to use as are sent up to us, such material as is given to God. This mansion represents what Harry Smith sent up, and the bungalow represents what you sent up."

At that, the rich woman awoke with a start.

Let's get busy doing God's will and furnishing materials for eternal glory.

Obey God. Do what He says. Be not slow to tell people of our

Saviour. Obey Him and do what He says because you belong to Him.

Let me review: Remember Lot's wife because there is a danger in looking back. Remember Lot's wife because the best is ahead. Remember Lot's wife because there is a dignity in obedience.

God grant that we shall obey our Saviour in this hour and do what He says.

12 The Geography of the Christian Life

"And after these things he went forth, and saw a publican, named Levi, sitting at the receipt of custom: and he said unto him, Follow me."—Luke 5:27.

"And it came to pass, that, as they went in the way, a certain man said unto him, Lord, I will follow thee whithersoever thou goest."—Luke 9:57.

The obedient Christian follows Christ anywhere. He does not hold back, does not hesitate. The geography of the Christian life includes obedience in all places.

The smooth places. Jesus took the disciples apart to rest. They followed Him and listened to His teaching. They enjoyed rest in the presence of our Saviour.

The stony places. There were times of sore disturbance. Some of the disciples wanted to call down fire upon their opponents, but Jesus led them in another way. We will all experience the stony places of life. Difficulties will be many.

The stormy places. There were times of deep distress. There was the occasion when the stormy winds came down upon the Sea of Galilee. When the disciples were in danger of losing their lives, it was then that Jesus came walking on water. He stilled the waves and spoke peace to their hearts.

I repeat: The geography of the Christian life will include obedience in all places, whether they be smooth, stony or stormy. At times you may have to travel the hills of severe persecution—such persecution as Jesus suffered in Nazareth and in Jerusalem. Be ready to suffer for His sake.

Again, be ready to go to the Garden of Gethsemane. There are lessons of suffering and submission to be learned, and these can come only in Gethsemane. They may be unpleasant but necessary experiences to the growing Christian.

We must come to the hill called Calvary and view the scene of our Saviour's death. We cannot die as He died, but we can be aware of the payment made for our redemption. We can rejoice that our Saviour is walking by our side.

Something else quite important and essential to the abundant Christian life—dying to self. The cross will bring us vividly to grips with this essential—the dying to self: death to the flesh, to our ambitions, to the inclinations of the flesh.

It should be our desire to follow Jesus anywhere He leads us—to the mountain tops or into the valleys, upon land or upon sea. As we follow Him, we will become deepened in our spiritual life and be led in greater accomplishments for our Master.

What does it mean to follow Christ? It means

I. RESIGNATION TO HIS WILL

The greatest prayer you can ever pray is: "Father, Thy will be done." Do not think that this prayer is easy. The words may be easy to say, but the thought is difficult to execute.

The Apostle Paul's life is an illustration of resignation to the will of God. When Christ met him on the road to Damascus, Paul said, "Lord, what wilt thou have me to do?" This question typifies the apostle's life. He was always ready for God to have His way. He was actively resigned to the will of God.

You say, "I would like to be like Paul." We will all join you in this. We would like to be like him, but it is more than mere words. When we begin to follow the Lord, even as Paul followed Him, a number of things must be considered.

Would I like the homelessness? Paul was homeless.

Would I like the hatred of my own people? Paul was hated.

Would I like the privations and the persecutions? Paul was

persecuted, stoned, cast out of cities.

Would I like the insecurity? From the human side, Paul had no security. He was resting upon the Lord.

Now, if I am willing to take on all these things, then I am ready to be like Paul and follow my Lord.

However, let me give this word of encouragement. The Lord does not lay upon you all trials at one time. He allows them to come one at a time so that you can better stand them.

Paul's being resigned to the will of God was not a dull giving over to the Lord, but an active meeting with God—a meeting with and a resignation to His will.

To follow Christ means

II. ACCEPTANCE OF HIS PLAN FOR YOUR LIFE

To follow Christ, there must be a resignation of your will to His, an acceptation of His plan for your life.

God's plan for you will not be discovered by jumping hither and yon. It will be given as you wait upon Him in quiet submission.

God's plan for Adoniram Judson's life meant a ministry in the land of Burma—the land of darkness, idolatry and cruelty. Judson walked in and undertook to overthrow Buddhism and to take the country for Christ. He translated the Bible into Burmese amid persecutions, cholera and smallpox.

He labored seven years before he baptized his first convert. For twenty-one months he was in prison with one hundred fierce criminals in a small room twenty by forty feet, with no ventilation, no sanitation, on starvation rations, with daily anticipation of death, and with fourteen pounds of chains on his arms and legs.

Judson had accepted God's plan for his life, and this was it. He suffered for Christ. He did not complain. For thirty-two years he literally gave himself to preach Christ, the Saviour of the world.

Before Judson left Boston, he had been offered a pastorate—a place of comfort and ease; but he declined to take the pastorate because God had said, "I want you in Burma."

What was the result of following the will of God? This is the result in part: "At his death he had oversight of 163 missionaries and nationals—one church of 7,000 members and 30,000 Christian communicants."

When David Livingstone accepted God's will for his life, it meant Africa. He gave himself wholly and completely to the Saviour, and the Lord led him day by day.

After a lifetime of suffering and hardships, he died in Africa. His body was placed among the illustrious dead in Westminster Abbey as a tribute to his tenacity of purpose, his scorn of obstacles, his rugged independence.

We need men like Livingstone—men who will stand when all others are failing and falling, men who are willing to suffer.

When George Mueller of Bristol accepted God's plan for his life, it meant eventually the keeping of five large orphanages, a circulating religious library, the sending out of hundreds of missionaries, and the teaching of 120,000 people in his schools. All of this cost one million, five hundred thousand pounds; yet Mr. Mueller never made a subscription list or an appeal for money.

D. L. Moody met God and testified as follows:

> I have never lost sight of Jesus Christ since the first day I met Him in the store at Boston. But for years I was only a nominal Christian, really believing that I could not work for God. No one had ever asked me to do anything.
>
> When I went to Chicago, I hired five pews in the church. I used to go out in the street and pick up young men and fill the pews. I never spoke to those young men about their souls. That was the work of the elders, I thought.
>
> After working some time like that, I started a mission Sunday school. I thought numbers were everything, and so I worked for numbers. When the attendance ran below one thousand, it troubled me. When it ran to twelve or fifteen hundred, I was elated. Still, none were converted. There was no harvest. Then God opened my eyes.

That is the story of the beginning of the ministry of D. L. Moody, one of the greatest preachers this world has ever known.

Whoever you are, whatever may be your life, your talents, your plans, to follow Jesus Christ means an acceptance of His plan for your life. For you it may mean a number things. Here are some things it will surely mean.

First, it will mean giving—the giving of yourself, the giving of all you have unto the Lord. Oh, that we might consider everything we have as coming from the Lord and unselfishly let go of it all if God so requires.

In Gloucester, England, there is an old-fashioned garden. In one corner is a little tombstone. On it are the following words:

December 21, 1869

> Here lies Tidman's missionary hen. Her contributions—four pounds, ten shillings. Although she is dead, the work goes on, as she left seven daughters and a son to carry on the work that she begun.

A man named Tidman lived in a village nearby. He longed to do something for the London Missionary Society; but since money was scarce, he decided that one of his hens should belong to the Society and that all the eggs she laid should be sold and the money given for Christian work.

Before the hen died, the money amounted to four pounds, ten shillings, about $10.00.

But that was not all. Tidman hatched out eight of the eggs. These, too, belonged to the Society, and in due time brought a sizeable sum of money.

When the hen died, her body was embalmed and buried in the garden, with a monument erected at her grave.

A strange story, but an illustration that all we have and all we are should be given to our Saviour.

Second, accepting God's plan for your life will mean letting your light shine so that others may see and know that you are a child of God.

Third, it will mean serving. You will be busy for Christ every day. Whatever the task, you will do it for Him and for His glory.

Fourth, it will mean witnessing. Jesus said, "Ye shall be witnesses unto me." Our task is to witness to others. There is no exception to this call of God. All are to be witnesses—preachers, deacons, people.

Yes, to follow Jesus will mean accepting His plan for you. Don't be foolish. Don't turn away from the thing God has desired of you. To follow Christ means

III. DESIGNATION OF ALL GLORY TO HIM

There are three simple words which I want you to keep in mind.

First, resignation to His will; second, acceptation of His plan; third, designation of all glory to Him.

No one is going to say this is easy. Self is so strong that it will take glory to itself, but we must say, "Lord, let Thy name be glorified in what I do."

Are you living according to His will? Then let the glory be His.

Are you living as He has planned for you? Then be sure that you give all glory to Him. Let His name be glorified through your life.

In Acts 12 is the sad story of Herod, a man who took glory to himself. He sat before the people, made an oration unto them, and the people shouted, "It is the voice of a god, and not of man." What does the Word say? "And immediately the angel of the Lord smote him, because he gave not God the glory: and he was eaten of worms, and gave up the ghost."

How different it was with the Apostle Paul! In the closing days of his life, as given in II Timothy 4, we find him glorifying God: "The Lord stood with me in the time of trial." "The Lord shall deliver me from every evil work." He closed the letter by saying, "The Lord Jesus Christ be with thy spirit. Grace be with you. Amen."

Let this be your motto: "My best for His glory."

We have no promise of an easy way, but we do have the promise of His constant, daily presence.

> God hath not promised
> Skies always blue,
> Flower-strewn pathways
> All our lives through.
> God hath not promised
> Sun without rain,
> Joy without sorrow,
> Peace without pain.
>
> But God hath promised
> Strength for the day,

Rest from the labor,
Light for the way,
Grace for the trials,
Help from above,
Unfailing sympathy,
Undying love.

Right now will you lay your life upon the altar and tell Him, "Lord, take my life and use it for Thy glory"?

When you surrender your all to Him, He will not fail you.

13 The Value of One Hour

"And he cometh unto the disciples, and findeth them asleep, and saith unto Peter, What, could ye not watch with me one hour?"—Matt. 26:40.

Two thoughts press in on me as I consider this text: first, the scene of Gethsemane and its meaning; and second, the preciousness of time as emphasized by our Saviour.

In a moment we shall deal with the matter of Gethsemane, but consider now the matter of time.

We are guilty, all of us, of wasting time! There are many simple truths about time which escape our attention.

Time is God-given, and it must not be wasted. We have all the same amount of time—sixty minutes to the hour, twenty-four hours in a day, seven days per week.

Time is short. Said Paul in I Corinthians 7:29, "But this I say, brethren, the time is short...."

Someone has estimated that, in the average life of seventy years, time would be used up as follows: three years spent in education, eight years in amusements, six years at the dinner table, five years in transportation, four years in conversation, fourteen years in work, three years in reading, twenty-four years in sleeping, three years in convalescing.

(Someone made this comment on time: The person who attends a ninety-minute religious service each Sunday and who prays ten minutes each morning would be giving only ten months—not even a full year—out of seventy years.)

Time is uncertain. "For what is your life? It is even a vapour, that appeareth for a little time, and then vanisheth away" (James 4:14).

Time must not be wasted. Wasted hours never return. Time is one commodity that cannot be replaced.

> **The clock of time is wound but once;**
> **And no man has the power**
> **To tell just when the hands will stop—**
> **At late or early hour.**
> **Now is the only time you own.**
> **Live, love, toil with a will.**
> **Place no faith in tomorrow, for**
> **The clock may then be still.**

Youth, be aware of time. The wise man said, "Remember now thy Creator in the days of thy youth, while the evil days come not, nor the years draw nigh, when thou shalt say, I have no pleasure in them."

Now I bid you to return to the scene in the Garden of Gethsemane.

I. THE PLAINTIVE CRY

"What, could ye not watch with me one hour?" This cry came from the lips of the Son of God when He found Peter, James and John sleeping in one of the most crucial hours of the Saviour's life. He gave the cry to Peter and said, "Watch and pray, that ye enter not into temptation: the spirit indeed is willing, but the flesh is weak."

Jesus went back to His place of prayer and prayed, "O my Father, if it be possible, let this cup pass from me: nevertheless not as I will, but as thou wilt" (Matt. 26:39).

He came again to the three and found them sleeping. He prayed again the third time, saying the same words. He came again and found them asleep, and this time He said:

"Sleep on now, and take your rest: behold, the hour is at hand, and the Son of man is betrayed into the hands of sinners. Rise, let us be going: behold, he is at hand that doth betray me."—Matt. 26:45,46.

Christ was the Son of God, but He was also the Son of man. He came to die upon the cross. He came to suffer for us; and how He did suffer!

It was suffering when He looked upon the multitude and said, "The harvest truly is plenteous, but the labourers are few." When the Saviour saw the crowds, "He was moved with compassion on them, because they fainted, and were scattered abroad, as sheep having no shepherd."

It was suffering when He looked upon Jerusalem and said:

"O Jerusalem, Jerusalem, thou that killest the prophets, and stonest them which are sent unto thee, how often would I have gathered thy children together, even as a hen gathereth her chickens under her wings, and ye would not!"—Matt. 23:37.

It was suffering when Jesus ". . . beheld the city, and wept over it" (Luke 19:41).

It was suffering when from the cross He cried out, "My God, my God, why hast thou forsaken me?"

Now think again of this plaintive cry coming from our Saviour as He said to Peter, "What, could ye not watch with me one hour?"

This cry indicates the seriousness of His sufferings. This portrays in part some of the agony of the Garden of Gethsemane. Remember, He had said to the three, "My soul is exceeding sorrowful even unto death: tarry ye here, and watch." No one can fully understand the acute sufferings of the Son of God as He prayed in the Garden of Gethsemane.

I think that this plaintive cry also indicates the Saviour's understanding of our burdens. After praying three times and coming back to the disciples, He finally said, "Sleep on now, and take your rest. . . ."

Jesus was not without awareness of the weakness of man. He understood the pressures that were placed upon these disciples. But at the same time, His heart cried out, "What, could ye not watch with me one hour?"

II. THE PLAIN CAUSE

Read the plaintive cry again, and you will see the cause: He found the disciples asleep. The cause of His cry: sleeping disciples.

Tired? Yes. They had gone through many rigorous hours with Christ. Dangers were lurking in many places, and they were conscious of them. All of this exhausted them so that, when Jesus went aside to pray, they went to sleep.

You may try to excuse them, but you can't escape the cry of Christ: "What, could ye not watch with me one hour?"

Gethsemane was a crucial hour, an hour of intense anguish for the Saviour. These men were His closest disciples. They had been with Him on other great occasions. And the record indicates that, on one of them, they had behaved very much like men: Peter, James and John went to sleep on the Mount of Transfiguration.

But this was such a momentous occasion, it is hard to imagine men going to sleep. It seems that Gethsemane called for a special effort, but they did not give it. Christ is calling for people to go a little farther.

This day calls for a special effort. Will we give it?—this day of deepening sin, this day of colossal indifference, this day of woeful ignorance, this day of lowering standards, this day of lessened respect for holiness, this day of foolish emphasis on nonessentials.

Both youth and age must work on.

First, selfishness is condemned by the Scriptures. Paul said of the people in his day, "For all seek their own, and not the things which are Jesus Christ's."

It is inspiring to read about people who live for others. John Wesley was such a one.

If you recall the story, this man served God for fifty-three years after his heartwarming Aldersgate conversion. He went across England preaching the Gospel. He was master of six languages and was thoroughly versed in theology, history and literature. Physically he was unimpressive, standing five feet four inches tall, weighing less than 130 pounds. But with seemingly boundless energy, he preached 40,000 sermons, traveled 250,000 miles (mostly on horseback), and wrote 400 books and pamphlets. His audiences sometimes numbered 20,000, which he held spellbound without public address systems.

After a vigorous, unselfish life, Wesley died at age 87. The story of Wesley surely condemns the selfishness of this hour.

I was reading the other day about a soldier boy who did an unselfish thing and received a great return from God.

A young soldier by the name of Page was stationed in Egypt during World War II. When payday came, he put his tithe in an envelope and sent it to his mother. On one occasion he said, "Give it to the preacher. Tell him I want us to have a new Sunday school building so that, when I get home, I can have a Sunday school room and not have to be in a class that has to sit in the auditorium. All in our class have wished for a room of our own."

Two years later, when the war was over, the boy started home. He called his mother and told her what train he would be on. Nearly a thousand people were at the station to meet him. He didn't think the crowd came to meet him, so he began looking to see who was behind him, whom all these people had come to meet.

His mother was in front of him, along with the preacher, a crowd of the deacons and others. After they had greeted him, they said, "Now before you go home, we are going to take you by the church. There is something we want you to see."

They stopped the car in front of a beautiful educational building. Lo, and behold, carved in marble above the door was THE PAGE BUILDING.

He stood there astonished and confused; then he began to weep. Finally he asked, "Why did they name it after me?" The preacher answered, "I read to the congregation one Sunday morning that letter you wrote to your mother. I held up the dollar bills that you sent in your letter. The church took it from there. That letter, those dollar bills and your faithful stewardship built that building. Your name belongs on it."

Second, thoughtlessness is condemned by the Scriptures. We must remember who we are and what God has called us to do. There must be about us a constant alertness to the situations facing us. We must give our best to the Saviour.

Third, indifference is condemned by the Scriptures—indifference toward the church, indifference toward your Christian obligations, indifference toward soul winning, indifference toward missions, indifference toward prayer. This is condemned by the words of our Saviour, "What, could ye not watch with me one hour?"

I am always listening for words that indicate strength of character and inner determination.

On last evening as I shook hands with many people in a church about a hundred miles from here, a little lady came up and said, "I have prayed for my husband for fourteen years almost night and day. But I will not stop. I will not give up. I will pray until I see him saved or until death takes me Home."

May God awaken our hearts to the great task which is ours. May we not fail to throw our best into the service of Christ!

III. THE POSITIVE CURE

We have talked about, first, the plaintive cry; second, the plain cause; now, the positive cure.

To use our lives correctly, we must face certain things.

First, we must examine our love for Christ. In that beautiful little portion of the Word of God in John 21:15-17, Jesus questioned Simon Peter: "...lovest thou me more than these?..." Examine your love for Christ. Do you love Him more than all the things of this world?

Above all else, I want to live a Christ-centered life. It is when our eyes are centered upon the Saviour that amazing and wonderful things happen.

One of the greatest hymns ever written was composed in less than five minutes. It has now lived for more than eighty years.

George Matheson had been in darkness for more than twenty years. When his eyesight vanished, his fiancee rejected him, his plans turned to ashes, and his horizon paled into blackness.

On the day that his sister was being married, he didn't go to the wedding; but he thought upon his twenty years in darkness.

It had been a score of years since he had seen the lovely smile of his mother. It had been twenty years since he had beheld the glories of a golden sunrise or the radiance of a colorful sunset. He was a young man when he saw his last rainbow wrap itself around the neck of a dying storm.

But on that day George Matheson, with a heart centered on serving God, was inspired. He seized his pen and wrote blindly for less than five minutes. From the inner sources of his heart he produced a masterpiece:

> O Love that wilt not let me go,
> I rest my weary soul in Thee;
> I give Thee back the life I owe,
> That in Thine ocean depths its flow
>   May richer, fuller be.
>
> O Light that follow'st all my way,
> I yield my flick'ring torch to Thee.
> My heart restores its borrowed ray,
> That in Thy sunshine's blaze its day
>   May brighter, fairer be.

He thought about Love and Light. Then he saw the suffering of the Lord Jesus. He seems to have sensed the driving of the nails into His hands and feet. He envisioned Christ saying, "It is finished." Then he penned these words:

> O Joy that seekest me thru pain,
> I cannot close my heart to Thee.
> I trace the rainbow thru the rain
> And feel the promise is not vain
>   That morn shall tearless be.

When he came to the final stanza, his heart was fixed upon the cross. Here is what he wrote:

> O Cross that liftest up my head,
> I dare not ask to fly from Thee.
> I lay in dust, life's glory dead,
> And from the ground there blossoms red
>   Life that shall endless be.

The Christ-centered life of a man who had been blind for twenty years produced a masterpiece in less than five minutes.

Second, we must die to self. The cure for selfishness, thoughtlessness and indifference will take place when we die to our own desires.

"Likewise reckon ye also yourselves to be dead indeed unto sin, but alive unto God through Jesus Christ our Lord."—Rom. 6:11.

"For ye are dead, and your life is hid with Christ in God."—Col. 3:3.

Self is your great enemy. Satan is ever working. The demons of Hell are trying to overthrow your life. So live for Him. Reckon self to be dead.

Third, we must set a high standard for faithfulness. Set it yourself! I could set it for you, but it will never stick unless you set it for yourself.

Joshua and Caleb believed God and were faithful. They alone felt that the Promised Land could be conquered and possessed. For their faithfulness they received the hatred of their kinsmen.

Nehemiah was faithful. Men desired his life and attempted to destroy his work.

Here is the positive cure. First, we must examine our love for Christ; second, we must die to self; third, we must set a high standard of faithfulness. Give more time to the Word of God, more time for prayer, more time for witnessing to the lost.

A young man was offered a job in Boston and was packing to leave. His mother said, "Son, there is a picture in a department store that I want you to see." The young man pleaded that he didn't have time to do this. Then his mother said as she put her arms about him, "Son, you will soon be gone. I won't be able to ask you for any more favors. Please do this for me."

"All right," he said, "if you put it that way."

They went to the store and pushed open the door of a certain room. There in the darkened room, under a shaft of light, he saw a man on his knees praying. The son moved a little closer and saw that it was a picture, a picture so wonderful and so beautiful that his heart was touched and stirred.

He didn't enjoy the party that he attended that night. He couldn't get the picture out of his mind.

The next day he said, "Mother, let's go and see that picture again." They went to the store and into the room. After looking at the picture for a long time, he said, "Mother, why is he so sad? Why are his hands so pleading?"

She answered, "Son, that's Jesus praying in Gethsemane. He is thinking of those for whom He is going to die. He is thinking of the multitudes who will need to know of His death. He is praying for God to raise up men and women to tell His story."

The young man bowed his head and said, "Blessed Lord! If anything is left undone that I can do, You can count on me."

I want you to look again at this garden scene and hear the voice of Jesus saying, "What, could ye not watch with me one hour?"

Could He be speaking to some of us who have turned away from the place of duty? Could He be appealing to some who have forsaken the task of soul winning? Could He be pleading with some who have given up their daily Bible reading and prayer life?

Will you say right now, "I surrender my all to Him. I give Him my life, everything I have"?

14 Inspection Day for Highland Park Baptist Church

"And Jesus entered into Jerusalem, and into the temple: and when he had looked round about upon all things, and now the eventide was come, he went out unto Bethany with the twelve."—Mark 11:11.

Do you live in the consciousness of the presence of Christ? Remember—He is both watching us and watching over us.

He knows everything about us. Nothing is hidden from Him. He knows our successes, our failures.

He knows about our giving. How dare we give selfishly! How dare we accept any basis of giving that is not scriptural!

He knows about our witnessing. His command has been given: "Ye shall be witnesses unto me." It is ours to obey! If we disobey, we lose.

As He knows about us individually, so does He know about this church. He knew all about the seven churches of Asia Minor. He knows about every church in this city, this state, this nation, this world.

May God awaken us to His presence in our midst. We must answer to Him. If I can make you think of Christ and His presence in our midst, this will change what you are thinking and how you are acting.

I have been watching and talking to Christians for a long time. I notice you Christians in our church and observe your response to the things I say.

Some Christians decide how often they will go to church, disregarding every scriptural exhortation and every pulpit admonition.

Some decide how they will serve God, no matter what the Bible says and no matter what others may say or do.

Some decide how they will give, despite the Bible teachings and testimonies to the blessings of tithing.

Inspection day! "And Jesus entered into Jerusalem and into the temple: and when he had looked round about upon all things...." Think of the Son of God walking into our church and looking upon us. There will certainly be many things that He would approve and disapprove.

Three things I trust He will find.

May Christ

I. FIND US PREACHING THE WHOLE COUNSEL OF GOD

I believe the Bible from the first word of Genesis to the last word of Revelation! Not a single line, not a verse, not a chapter, not a story, not a miracle, not a parable would I omit from the Word! This is God's Book, and I believe it.

Now it is my business to preach the Word of God. I am to declare the message that God has given.

First, preach on the work of the local church. God has ordained that the work of this age be carried on by churches. God has given His command as to what we are to do: to preach the message of Christ and to declare the work of His church.

We have no Bible commands about the erecting of buildings; we have no Bible teachings regarding the organization of training unions or Sunday schools or girls' auxiliaries or Royal Ambassadors; but we do have His definite command regarding the work of the local church in Matthew 28:18-20:

"And Jesus came and spake unto them, saying, All power is given unto me in heaven and in earth.

"Go ye therefore, and teach all nations, baptizing them in the name of the Father, and of the Son, and of the Holy Ghost:

"Teaching them to observe all things whatsoever I have commanded you: and, lo, I am with you alway, even unto the end of the world. Amen."

Our Lord's command here has been both disobeyed and disregarded by many. Some churches will recognize that this is His Word to us and this is our work, but they still do nothing.

Some people disregard this plain command of Christ altogether. I am thinking now of the many denominations around us. Some have magnificent buildings, but there is no program of evangelism and missions. It is my business to preach about the work of the local church.

Second, preach the prophecies of this Book. This means giving constant emphasis to the second coming of our Saviour. He said, "I will come again, and receive you unto myself." We must not come short in declaring this message. We must not be timid in saying again and again, "Christ is coming!"

The truth of the second coming of Christ should cause us to be clean in life. After John spoke about the second coming of Christ, he said, "And every man that hath this hope in him purifieth himself, even as he is pure" (I John 3:3).

The second coming of Christ means we will be called upon to stand before the judgment seat of Christ and there to give an account of ourselves unto God. Paul said, ". . . for we shall all stand before the judgment seat of Christ" (Rom. 14:10). Again he said, "For we must all appear before the judgment seat of Christ; that every one may receive the things done in his body, according to that he hath done, whether it be good or bad" (II Cor. 5:10).

We are to preach also the millennial reign of Christ, that we are going to reign with Christ upon this earth for a thousand years. Paul said, "Do ye not know that the saints shall judge the world? and if the world shall be judged by you, are ye unworthy to judge the smallest matters?" (I Cor. 6:2).

Then we must tell lost sinners there is coming a great white throne judgment, pictured in Revelation 20:11-15. This is the time when the lost dead will stand before the judgment and receive their sentence into the lake of fire. Verse 12 says, "And I saw the dead, small and great, stand before God; and the books were opened: and another book was opened, which is the book of life: and the dead were judged out of those things which were written in the books, according to their works."

Yes, it is our obligation to preach the prophecies of the Bible and to point people to the Saviour and the events related to His coming.

Third, preach on consecration and separation. This is the message of the entire Word of God. It is found in every book of the Bible, from Genesis to Revelation. In II Corinthians 6:17 are the words, "Wherefore come out from among them, and be ye separate, saith the Lord, and touch not the unclean thing; and I will receive you."

These and many other truths are to be preached. As Christ walks in our midst, may He find us preaching the whole counsel of God. Don't turn away from subjects that may not be popular, but preach the whole message. Talk about salvation. Talk about Heaven and Hell. Declare unto men the way whereby they must be saved.

I can never forget the revival meeting that I conducted in a large Baptist church in Birmingham, Alabama. God blessed in a mighty way, and souls were saved.

One evening the pastor took me aside and said, "I must confess a mistake that I made. When this church called me as pastor, they made a request that I preach the Bible but omit any preaching on Hell. They stated that the former pastor had preached on Hell so much that they were tired of the subject."

He told me that he did not preach on Hell and had not done so for a number of years.

In the course of my meeting, I had preached often upon the subject and had dealt with the matters of judgment and damnation. Many souls had been saved. His own heart had been troubled because he had turned away from declaring the whole counsel of God.

May the living Christ

II. FIND US WORKING IN THE POWER
OF THE HOLY SPIRIT

Not our power, but His!

Yes, He is walking in our midst! But are we working in His power?

"Not by might, nor by power, but by my spirit, saith the Lord of hosts."—Zech. 4:6.

"But ye shall receive power, after that the Holy Ghost is come upon you: and ye shall be witnesses unto me both in Jerusalem, and in all Judaea, and in Samaria, and unto the uttermost part of the earth."— Acts 1:8.

"And be not drunk with wine, wherein is excess; but be filled with the Spirit."—Eph. 5:18.

This is a day of such frivolity and foolishness! This is the day when it is hard to get anyone to think seriously about the subject before us.

Publicity is given to a great organization at the University of California. A group called "The Headquarters of World Happiness" is engaged in passing out bubble gum. On a certain day they hoped to unite all of the nine campuses of the University of California for a great day in chewing bubble gum! One of the group members says that blowing bubbles brings happiness.

I mention that only as an example of the foolishness of this hour. We have turned away from serious contemplation on the things of God.

Think with me! The Spirit indwells the believer. When the church has power, it means Christians are full of the Holy Spirit. Souls are won by Spirit-filled believers.

I saw these two paragraphs the other day written by Dr. R. G. Lee:

> The lowest temperature authentically recorded in the United States was 65 degrees below zero, Fahrenheit, at Fort Keough, now Miles City, Montana, in January, 1888.
>
> I wonder how low the temperature inside our churches would be if it were measured by our spiritual passion for the lost or by missionary zeal. A thermometer would have a hard struggle to stay above zero if the mercury in it moved according to the real concern for sin-damned and Hell-doomed sinners around us—sometimes under the same roof with us—sometimes in the same office with us—sometimes dining at the same table with us.

Second, missionary programs are inaugurated by the Holy Spirit working in the local church. This is surely pictured in Acts 13. The Christians met together in Antioch; and as they prayed, the Holy Spirit said, "Separate me Barnabas and Saul for the work whereunto I have called them."

If young people are not volunteering for mission work, then we are not praying nor seeking the leadership of the Holy Spirit.

Third, the light of the church shines farthest when the members are under the direction of the Holy Spirit. Highland Park Baptist Church should so shine daily that every person in Chattanooga knows of our existence. We must so live and so conduct ourselves that there will be no doubt in the minds of people regarding what we are and what we are doing.

What a dream! Pastors and members filled with the Holy Spirit! What miracles would take place, what accomplishments would occur for the glory of God!

Yes, I say unto you that I trust the living Christ will walk among us and inspect us and find us working in the power of the Holy Spirit.

Again, may Christ

III. FIND US FOCUSING ON THE MAIN TASK

We are to "Preach the Word; be instant in season, out of season, reprove, rebuke, exhort with all longsuffering and doctrine" (II Tim. 4:2).

Eight words seem to describe the condition of this hour.

No vision. The Bible says, "Where there is no vision, the people perish." Churches and denominations have lost the vision. They fail to see that our primary task is to bring people into a saving relationship with the Lord Jesus Christ.

We exist for one great purpose: the giving of the Gospel to a lost world. Someone said, "The church does not primarily exist on behalf of itself but on behalf of the world." I am afraid that we have lost this idea and, hence, have lost the vision of a needy world.

Few workers. The Saviour said in Matthew 9:37, "The harvest truly is plenteous, but the labourers are few." Few are willing. Few are trained. Few are faithful. In spite of all of our churches, schools, colleges, universities, we have but few workers.

Little faith is the third great problem of this hour. Men are afraid to step out in the fields of service. What Jesus said to the people of His day must be said to many in this day, "O ye of little faith."

Baby Christians. "And, I brethren, could not speak unto you as unto spiritual, but as unto carnal, even as unto babes in Christ" (I Cor. 3:1). So many have failed to "grow in grace and in the knowledge of our Lord and Saviour, Jesus Christ."

No vision—few workers—little faith—baby Christians—here is the summary of our problem.

But God is calling us to focus upon the main task.

I frequently stand at the window of our home and, with field glasses, look toward Lookout Mountain, a historic spot. Often when I pick up the glasses, they are out of focus. The mountain is fuzzy and indistinct. I see only a blur. But when I bring the glasses into focus, I see the incline with cars going up and down the side of the mountain.

The modern church has lost her focus. Most of the modern churches are trying too many things. Some of them focus on the social gospel instead of on the eternal, spiritual Gospel of saving grace. Too many focus on reputation, on finances, on organization, on buildings. Some focus on theology.

First, we must focus on man's need. Man is a sinner, lost and undone. "For all have sinned, and come short of the glory of God" (Rom. 3:23).

We must focus on Christ and His death. The center of the gospel story is this: Christ died for our sins, according to the Scriptures. Men and women, boys and girls must see the death of Jesus for sinners. They must know that salvation comes in just one way—by resting upon the atoning death of our Saviour.

We must focus on compassion. How often we read these beautiful words about our Saviour: "And Jesus was moved with compassion. . . ."

Have you failed in soul winning? Have you just about given up this primary task? Do you feel that it is impossible to win others to Christ?

I like this story about the boy, Roy Ruggles. Roy was a football player playing at a Rose Bowl game. He recovered a fumble and raced the wrong way. He carried the ball through the goal posts of the opposing team, not realizing for a few moments that he had made this awful mistake. It was the last play of the first half of the game.

Years later Roy Ruggles tells us what he did. In substance he said:

> When I realized what I had done, I took off for the dressing rooms, thoroughly humiliated. When I got there, I went over to a corner, fell flat on my face on the floor. As the team came in, nobody spoke to me. They all gathered at the other end of the room. I beat my fists against the floor and said over and over again, "I'll never throw another football as long as I live!"
>
> The coach came in and began to give instructions to the team for the second half. About two minutes before time for them to go back onto the field, he called my name. I didn't even look up or answer him until he called it again in a very stern voice. "Get up off that floor and come here!"
>
> As I went over to him with my head bowed in shame, he said a most surprising thing, "Roy, their team is stronger on the left side, so I want you to go out and play the right halfback position against the strong side."
>
> All the words I could get out were, "But, but . . . ."
>
> Then he silenced me with this never-to-be-forgotten sentence: "The game is just half over. Go play it like I know you can."
>
> As we ran out to take our positions, the announcer said with astonishment in his voice, "Roy Ruggles is back on the field." A little later the announcer was yelling again, "Roy Ruggles is carrying the ball. He is making the best broken-field running I ever saw. He runs like he has wings to help him. They can't catch him. He will go all the way!" Then the roar of the applause drowned out the announcer's voice.

Simon Peter failed, but Christ gave him renewed zeal and compassion for a lost world. He went back to tell the story of Jesus.

Let me review. What is our need? to focus on man's need, to focus on Christ's death, to focus on compassion for souls.

What does every church need?

First, the presence of Christ. Thank God, He is willing and ready to help us!

Second, the power of Christ. He said to the disciples, "All power is given unto me in heaven and in earth. Go ye therefore . . . ."

His power has been given unto us.

Third, the purpose of Christ. "Christ Jesus came into the world to save sinners, of whom I am chief," said the Apostle Paul.

Fourth, the peace of Christ. Jesus said, "My peace I give unto you." The peace of God will be with us as we obey our Saviour.

There is peace in believing, peace in serving, peace in trusting our Saviour.

In the *Reader's Digest* of a few years ago, there appeared a most unforgettable story. Dr. Maxwell Maltz told of an Italian by the name of Cremona. Cremona was a barber in the section where he lived, which was one of the worst sections of the slums of New York. Cremona was the idol of all the boys. His barbershop was clean and neat. There wasn't an ugly picture on the wall. They were all beautiful pictures—copies of the *Mona Lisa*, the crucifixion, the resurrection, the birth of Jesus.

Dr. Maltz said, "Often Cremona would stand at the door; and when one of us would go by, he would say, 'Come on in. Your hair needs cutting.'

" 'But I don't have any money.'

" 'Who said anything about money?' and he would cut our hair and, while he cut it, talk to us about the Lord Jesus Christ."

Dr. Maltz said that, when he grew up and became a doctor and a Christian, he specialized in plastic surgery.

One day his wife came up to see him and said, "Cremona wants to see you."

Dr. Maltz said, "After office hours I went over to his house. His welcome warmed my heart. He said, 'Great doctor, you have come to see Cremona.'

"I turned to his wife and said, 'Doctor and Cremona have things to talk about in secret.'

"When she was gone, he whispered, 'Doctor, come down closer. Doctor, Cremona has about finished his life. Cremona is going Home. Doctor, one thing Cremona wants you to do above everything else, please. I will pay you what I can.'"

Dr. Maltz said, "You have already paid me a hundred times over."

Cremona said, "Doctor, long years ago in Sicily, Cremona and another boy had a bad fight. Cremona cut the other boy up, and the other boy cut up Cremona. The big handle-bar mustache I wear is to cover the scar. Doctor, I am going to stand before my Maker soon, and I am ashamed of the scar. My mustache won't hide it from Him. Doctor, take the scar off before I die."

The doctor, already crying, said, "Where is this scar, Cremona?" He reached up and touched the face of Cremona and looked for the scar, but he couldn't see it. He said, "Cremona, are you sure that's the right place?"

"Yes, right down across the upper lip."

Dr. Maltz said, "I examined it carefully, but there was no scar."

At the end of that story in the *Reader's Digest,* Dr. Maltz added this word, "Now you can say what you want to, any of you who read this. You might say old age draws the skin tight and effaces some things. I say to you that Cremona was such a fine Christian that God took that scar off him."

I don't know anything about Cremona's scar, but I rejoice in relating this about one who witnessed for his Saviour and was ready to meet his God.

"Inspection Day for Highland Park Baptist Church." When Christ walks into our midst—He is here now—may He find us, first, preaching the whole counsel of God; second, working in the power of the Holy Spirit; and third, focusing on the main task.

I went to see one of our members yesterday. This dear one is over one hundred years of age. She said, "Are you praying for me?"

I said, "Oh, yes, I pray for you every day."

She talked for awhile about the church, about the Friendship Sunday School Class, and about the Lord. Then we had a prayer. We shook hands, and she said, "Good-bye, son."

I walked into the hallway and stood there for a moment. Tears came into my eyes. As I thought of this one, more than one hundred years old, weak in body but alert in mind, three words came to my lips—**so near Heaven!**

I beg you to come to the Lord Jesus Christ and receive Him as your Saviour. Christian friend, if there is anything between you and the Lord, make things right this day.

15   **Keep on Knocking**

"I say unto you, Though he will not rise and give him, because he is his friend, yet because of his importunity [persistency], he will rise and give him as many as he needeth."—Luke 11:8.

(Read Luke 11:1-10 and Luke 18:1-8.)

I want to pay tribute to persistent people. Thank God for Christians who pray and refuse to quit praying. You belong to the line of George Mueller, who prayed and God opened the windows of Heaven for him.

Mr. Mueller was a man of faith—a man who would not give up. You recall that he prayed daily for the salvation of two men. His time of praying extended for more than fifty years. And Mr. Mueller died without seeing them saved. But not long after his death, both men got saved. His persistence in prayer paid off.

Thank God for the Christians who faithfully witness and refuse to quit. This is the service that God blesses. Faithfulness receives a special commendation of our Lord. You may not do as much as someone else, but being faithful will bring its reward.

This story appeared in the bulletin of the Calvary Baptist Church, Covington, Kentucky, Warren Wiersbe, pastor:

A dedicated soul winner in South Carolina stepped up to a house and rang the doorbell. No one answered. He rang it again and again. In fact, he rang it six times before he heard any sounds on the other side.

An angry man opened the door, accepted the tract that was offered and slammed the door violently.

But a week later, when the soul winner returned to the house, this time the man answered the door immediately. He took the visitor to the attic and showed him a noose hanging from the rafters!

"Friend, my neck was in that noose when you rang the bell last week," he said. "You were so persistent that I came down the stairs and answered. I read your tract, and the Lord spoke to me. Now I am a saved man!"

That story gives emphasis to my subject title, "Keep on Knocking."

Recently I read a summary of the life of John Vassar, the soul winner. In one chapter, the author pointed out what he believed made John Vassar a great man. Here are the seven points which he gave:

First, his unflinching loyalty to the Lord Jesus. There was a friendship between the man and his Saviour. An irreverent mention of the Saviour's name would cause him keen distress. Or if a preacher failed to mention the name of Christ in a sermon, this distressed him.

Second, his habitual and almost unbroken contact with God in prayer. His friends said that he literally prayed without ceasing. He prayed about everything. He prayed everywhere. He prayed with everyone he met. His supplications were intense.

Third, he had a mighty faith. No place and no case seemed too hard or too hopeless for him to grapple with.

Fourth, John Vassar was tactful. He seldom made a blunder. He knew human nature. He could read men at a glance. He knew how to talk to the educator or the laboring man.

Fifth, he realized the worth of a soul. He saw every soul in need of Christ. At one time, when he was introduced to the President of the United States, he did not release his hand until he had asked him about his relationship to Jesus Christ. He was just as concerned for a little child as for an old man.

Sixth, his close adherence to the Word of God. He knew his Bible, and he used it. He had only one standard for his life—the Bible standard. He did not insist on his own notions or ideas, but he insisted on the Word of God.

Seventh, Uncle John possessed a remarkable persistency of purpose.

Zeal is sometimes flashy and fitful. But John Vassar was tenacious, persistent!

It is this that I am emphasizing in this message: persistency—keep on knocking!

When one is saved, he has a desire to win others to Christ. I think that salvation can well be questioned unless there is that desire to share what you have with others. If you have never had a desire to tell someone about Jesus, then you might well question the reality of your own experience.

But the tragedy is, so many start out right, then fade away. They do not keep on knocking at the hearts' doors of others.

A young man told me that he was deeply concerned for his lost father. "I witnessed to him once, but it seemed to anger him, so I never mentioned the matter again." That father may be wondering why his son does not speak to him again about this important matter.

The Bible surely indicates that, if we are going to be used by Him, we must be persistent in the work that He has given us to do. Without persistency, we are put on the shelf. We are on the sideline. We are useless.

On last Monday I drove by a score of railroad cars, derailed and piled up in a most grotesque way. They were useless until the mighty cranes could lift them back on the tracks again.

Christians are useless unless they are on the main track of service.

Now keep the illustration before you, the illustration of a man standing at a door knocking. After ringing six times, an angry man comes to the door, accepts the gospel tract given to him, slams the door violently; a week later the soul winner comes back to the house; this time the man brings him in, takes him to the attic, shows him the noose hanging from the rafters and says, "Friend, my neck was in that noose when you rang the bell last week. You were so persistent that I came down the stairs and answered. I read the gospel tract. The Lord spoke to me, and now I am a saved man!"

Now, I am emphasizing this matter—keep on knocking!

I. KEEP ON KNOCKING WITH THE EXAMPLE OF YOUR LIFE

Love in such a way that you are constantly impressing people

with the reality of Jesus Christ and with the transformation that
He can make in any life.

First, live a clean life. Turn away from all evil things, all doubtful things. Recognize that your body is the temple of the Holy Ghost
and that you have been bought with a price; therefore, you must
glorify God in your body and in your spirit, which are God's.

Remember the power of influence. Paul said, "No one lives to
himself, and no one dies to himself."

There is a striking story given about John Donne, one of the gifted
preachers and poets of the early seventeenth century. Someone said
of him: "He was a preacher in earnest, weeping sometimes for his
auditory and sometimes with them; always preaching to himself, like
an angel in the clouds."

Men who heard Donne speak always noted in him a vein of
sadness and melancholy—in truth as often said, "like an angel out
of the cloud." He preached unto himself, for he was shadowed and
haunted by the recollection of the licentious poems which he had
written with all the great talent that God has bestowed upon him—
poems calculated to sow the seeds of licentiousness and immorality
in other lives.

Those who have studied the life of John Donne testify that he
apparently never escaped the fact of his early sinfulness. His poems
were scattered everywhere; and when he became a preacher, he faced
much of his ministry in sorrow because of his early sinfulness.

I give that illustration to drive home to your heart the great need
for clean living. It is imperative that you young people live clean
so that your evil and sin will not haunt you in the latter part of life.

I emphasize clean living for mothers and fathers so that you need
not be ashamed for someone to see your life and to know what you are.

If we want to be soul winners, then one of the finest things we
can do is so live that others can see Christ in us.

Second, live courageously. Be strong and of a good courage. Let
others know of your convictions. Be unafraid to speak out and to tell
what you believe.

A Pittsburgh lawyer became desperately ill and was sent to the
hospital. On the night of his arrival, the physician who examined

him, alarmed at his condition, told him that he must have a stimulant at once, and prescribed whiskey.

The lawyer, who had been a total abstainer all of his life, said he would not take it.

The physician then had a private interview with the man's wife, saying that, unless her husband took the stimulant, he could not answer for his being alive on the morrow.

The wife answered, "You might as well try something else: you will carry him out of the hospital dead before he will take a drink of whiskey."

Another stimulant was given. In the course of a short time, the sick lawyer was on his road to recovery.

You see, the doctor who had prescribed the whiskey had had a very rugged career. He was the son of a brilliant father. The father tried to pull him out of his habit of strong drink, but failed. Again and again he would go back into this habit.

When the lawyer began to recover, the doctor came to him and said, "Sir, I owe you a great debt of gratitude. The night I tried to get you to take whiskey as a stimulant was one of those dangerous periods in my life. I was on the verge of surrendering to the old drinking habit again. But when you refused to drink, though it meant perhaps your death, it gave me courage to stand. Your refusal gave me a new determination."

This is courageous living! This Bible admonishes, "Be strong and of a good courage."

Third, live consistently. Live every day in the same way. Every day be on the job of living for Christ, showing His power, witnessing to His saving grace. God grant that our words, our appearance, our actions might all point to the Saviour.

The negative life hinders soul winning. The lukewarm Christian will never amount to much. He will never be a great power for righteousness.

Compromising churches do not excel in winning souls. They may get some crowds to come once every once in awhile, but they won't achieve in the main business unless the members are dedicated to living for Christ.

Now, I trust you will take this first point and apply it to your own life. Be an example by knocking on someone's door and pointing him or her to the Lord.

II. KEEP KNOCKING WITH YOUR TESTIMONY

First, does your testimony come from a fervent heart? This evil world will never be impressed by the cold and heartless. We may laugh at a fellow who gets excited and shouts out his testimony; but we must face the fact that he is doing something. Does it come from his heart? The cold Christian will never be a soul winner.

Second, base your testimony upon the Scripture. Don't be ashamed of the plain, biblical terms with regard to salvation. Tell people that you were a wicked sinner bound for Hell and that one day you heard the message of Christ, you repented of your sin, the sin of unbelief, and you received Christ as your Saviour.

Back up your testimony by chosen verses from the Word of God, such as John 1:12; 3:16; 3:36; Acts 4:12; Ephesians 2:8,9; and others.

Third, back your testimony by a dedicated life. Others are pointed to the Lord Jesus when they see Christ in you.

This is beautifully illustrated by the experience of Ted DeMoss. While in Toronto, Canada, he witnessed to a man, a church member but unsaved. He listened to Ted but did not accept the Lord Jesus on that occasion. Mr. DeMoss left his personal card with him.

Some time later this man called Chattanooga and asked for Ted DeMoss. He informed him that he was coming to Chattanooga and would bring his wife with him.

They arrived around 5:30 p.m. Before 6:00 p.m. Mr. Nelson Blount had accepted Jesus Christ as Saviour.

For the rest of his days, he gave a steady testimony to the grace of God. But, remember, it was the witness of a fervent Christian that caused him to see his lost condition and his need of Christ.

This Book says, "Ye shall be witnesses unto me." We are to keep on witnessing—in season, out of season.

We are to witness in the power of the Holy Spirit. This was true of the early Christians and must be true of us. Peter and John were unlearned men, but the enemy "took knowledge of them that they had been with Jesus." Under the fullness of the Holy Spirit's power, they witnessed and won souls.

III. KEEP ON KNOCKING WITH YOUR FERVENT PRAYERS

We are discussing soul winning in this message. I want you to see the importance of persistency, to see the necessity of continually knocking on doors and giving out the Gospel of Jesus Christ.

We have touched already on knocking with our example; second, knocking with our testimony; now, let us think about knocking with our fervent prayers.

First, pray for others with true gratitude of heart. Sometimes I am afraid our prayers are cold and lifeless because we don't have welling up within us gratitude for all that God has done for us.

Our soul winning often fails because we don't have that bright expression of gratitude. We fail to thank God for all He has done for us. We also fail to thank others who help us in so many ways.

A mother had reared six boys to manhood. She had done her best for the sons, and all had become outstanding men. Now the mother was on her deathbed. The boys came home to see her. The eldest, a powerful man, knelt by her side and, wiping the death dew from her forehead, said, "Mother, you have always been a good mother to us boys."

The tired mother closed her eyes. Great tears pushed out under the lids and ran down her wasted cheeks. Then she opened them, looked searchingly into the face of her son and said, "My boy, is that really true? Do you boys feel that way about me?"

He replied, "Indeed we do, Mother. We often speak of what a good mother you have been to us."

Again she closed her eyes, and great tears ran down her wasted cheeks. Then she opened them, looked into the face of her firstborn and said, "My boy, I prayed more that I might be a good mother to you six boys than anything else. I was afraid that I would fail in some way to be all I ought to be. I never knew whether you boys thought I had failed or not, until now. Not one of you ever told me I was a good mother until today."

It is somewhat of a tragedy that many of us fail to express our appreciation to others. We are not as grateful as we ought to be. We don't express our thanks to God as we should.

As you pray for others, make sure you pray with gratitude of heart. And as you knock upon the hearts' doors and invite men to the Saviour, make sure you do it with gratitude of heart.

Second, pray for fellow Christians. They need prayer—we all do.

Miss Amy Carmichael was a missionary in India. At the mission station where she did most of her work, they had a custom to pause on the hour for a few moments of prayer. Beautiful chimes would play, and for a few seconds all activity ceased. The people would bow their heads in meditation and pray for one another. So should we all. How sorely we need prayer! How sorely our fellow Christians need prayer!

> Please pray for me, my friends!
>   I need your prayers,
> For there are burdens pressing hard,
>   And many cares;
> Pray, too, that Christ will make of me
> The Christian that I ought to be!
>
> Do pray for me, my friend,
>   At morning hour,
> That I may not be overborne
>   By Satan's power;
> That, 'mid the whirl and maze of "things,"
> My soul may drink of hidden springs.
>
> Cease not to pray for me,
>   Though sundered far,
> Come, meet me at the mercy seat
>   From where you are;
> Nor time nor distance can divide
> Our hearts that in His love abide!
>
> Thus, praying each for each,
>   That will come true
> Of which our Lord and Master spake—
>   "If two of you"—(Matt. 18:19).
> No purer joy may friendship share
> Than in the fellowship of prayer!

Pray for the lost. My heart hungers to do what I have never done through all the years of my ministry. I pray for some lost people, but I never made it my business to pray for many by name. God has impressed me to pray that the unsaved will feel the convicting power of the Holy Spirit and turn to the Lord.

God gives us what we ask for. So begin now to ask for bigger things—for more souls to be saved, for a greater outreach of the Gospel of Jesus Christ. Spend more time in prayer for the services and for the salvation of the lost. Dr. William Ward Ayer said, "I would rather have fifty people on their knees on a Saturday night praying for the salvation of souls in my services on Sunday, than to have a page in the Saturday *New York Times*."

We have been talking about persistency—just keep on witnessing, knocking on hearts' doors everywhere.

In 1967 President Johnson sat for a portrait which was made by a famous artist. But the President was so displeased that he called it "the ugliest thing I ever saw."

A little later another portrait of him was painted by a lady artist of New York. The President was happy and satisfied with the new portrait.

The picture I have of myself is not a good one. It is a true one, for I believe that I know myself. I have failed the Lord so miserably in having a passion for souls. I have failed to keep on knocking at the door. I have been weak in pressing the message of Jesus Christ.

It may be that many of you have the same feeling about yourselves. It may be that you have given up all soul-winning activity. You have stopped talking to people about the Lord. Now your heart is troubled. Perhaps tonight God is calling you to a rededication of life and a renewal to soul winning.

In this invitation, I press upon the lost your need for salvation. I would like to knock upon your hearts' doors until you answer and receive the message. The heart of the Gospel is this: "Christ died for our sins, according to the scriptures." He only is able to save to the uttermost all who come to Him.

The old sawdust floor tabernacle used for four years: 1943–1947
(hot in the summer, cold in the winter)

Prayer services and Sunday school teachers and officers. In Phillips Chapel (the building when I became pastor of Highland Park Baptist Church in 1942)

A prayer service in 1973 in the Chauncey-Goode Auditorium. (Dr. Faulkner was leading singing. I am standing back of him.)

A picture made on Wednesday evening, April 27, 1983. My last service as pastor of Highland Park Baptist Church (in the new auditorium seating 6,000).

Picture of a prayer service, Wednesday, November 18, 1992. My 50th anniversary of coming to Chattanooga. (This picture was made by the *Chattanooga News—Free Press*.)

16 Lights on the Highway of Prophecy

"And beginning at Moses and all the prophets, he expounded unto them in all the scriptures the things concerning himself."—Luke 24:27.

From Adam to Christ—about four thousand years—there were lights of prophecy pointing to the coming of Christ, lights clear and unmistakable. Men of old read, understood and looked for His coming. We today read these Scriptures and see how clearly our Lord spoke of His coming into the world.

A few nights ago I was standing at a gate in an airport in Cleveland, Ohio, waiting to board my plane. Planes were landing rapidly and pulling into their places around the airport. Other planes were in the air waiting to land.

I turned to the attendant at the gate and asked, "Sir, do these lights on the planes mean anything to you? Can you tell what kind of plane is coming in by the lights?" He answered quickly, "Oh, yes. I can tell quite easily the type of plane that is coming to the field. In the night hours I know them by their lights."

We are living in the darkness of a sinful day. The strongest light we have is that shed abroad in our hearts by the Lord Jesus Christ.

Take your Bible and notice some of the prophecies regarding our Saviour.

I. THE PROPHECIES OF HIS FIRST COMING

In Luke 24 is an interesting story. Two men were walking on the road to Emmaus, about seven and one-half miles from Jerusalem. As they walked along, a "stranger" joined their company. They began to talk with Him regarding Jesus of Nazareth who had been crucified in Jerusalem. They told about the women who went to the sepulchre and found not His body.

Jesus saw that these two men were doubting; therefore,

"Then he said unto them, O fools, and slow of heart to believe all that the prophets have spoken:

"Ought not Christ to have suffered these things, and to enter into his glory?

"And beginning at Moses and all the prophets, he expounded unto them in all the scriptures the things concerning himself."

Don't you wish this full conversation had been recorded for us? However, we need not worry about what He said. This Word we have before us now. He certainly pointed them back to Genesis 3:15: "And I will put enmity between thee and the woman, and between thy seed and her seed; it shall bruise thy head, and thou shall bruise his heel."

It is quite certain that Jesus must have told the story as given in Numbers 21, of the brazen serpent that Moses made and put on a pole, when he said to the people, "Whosoever shall look upon this serpent shall live"; for we all know what Jesus said to Nicodemus:

"And as Moses lifted up the serpent in the wilderness, even so must the Son of man be lifted up: That whosoever believeth in him should not perish, but have eternal life."—John 3:14,15.

I imagine also that our Saviour must have pointed the two to the prophecies as given in Psalm 22. This Psalm tells us of the suffering Saviour, of His death upon the cross. It begins with the words, "My God, my God, why hast thou forsaken me?"—the very words that our Lord Jesus spoke upon the cross of Calvary.

He might also have pointed out the prophecies given in Zechariah 11:12 and 13, where it tells that Christ will be sold for thirty pieces of silver.

I think that we can be sure that the Son of God must have turned back to Isaiah 53 for definite quotations as He spoke to the two men who were slow of heart to believe.

He might also have referred to the Scripture in Micah 5 which tells of His birth in Bethlehem. He might have told of Isaiah 7:14 regarding His birth.

These and many other Scriptures were lights on the highway of prophecy, pointing men to the coming of our Saviour.

II. THE PROPHECIES OF HIS SECOND COMING

Do you believe in the first coming of Jesus Christ? Do you believe the prophecies which were given hundreds of years before His birth? Do you believe the literal fulfillment of these prophecies? You do? Then you must also believe in the prophecies of the coming of our Lord Jesus to this earth again. Jesus very plainly and pointedly said, "I will come again." One verse in every twenty-five in the New Testament refers to the coming of our blessed Lord.

"Therefore be ye also ready: for in such an hour as ye think not the Son of man cometh."—Matt. 24:44.

"Watch therefore, for ye know neither the day nor the hour wherein the Son of man cometh."—Matt. 25:13.

"When the Son of man shall come in his glory, and all the holy angels with him, then shall he sit upon the throne of his glory."—Matt. 25:31.

This Bible is full of the prophecies of the coming of our Lord. Remember the statement given by the two men in white apparel who stood by as Jesus ascended into the sky: "This same Jesus, which is taken up from you into heaven, shall so come in like manner as ye have seen him go into heaven."

The great Apostle Paul had no difficulty with this tremendous truth. In every portion of his writing we find reference to the coming of Christ. Listen to this:

"For our conversation is in heaven; from whence also we look for the Saviour, the Lord Jesus Christ: Who shall change our vile body, that it may be fashioned like unto his glorious body, according to the working whereby he is able even to subdue all things unto himself."—Phil. 3:20,21.

Every chapter in I Thessalonians ends with the promise of His coming. But one of the strongest passages is in I Thessalonians 4:13-18.

James was a preacher of the second coming. He said, "Be patient therefore, brethren, unto the coming of the Lord" (James 5:7).

The Apostle Peter was constantly preaching the second coming of Christ. Read in II Peter, chapter 3, where he tells us of the coming of the day of the Lord. He tells of the scoffers who are laughing at the promise of His coming. Then he goes on to say that the matter is established and that Christ is coming again.

The Apostle John believed firmly in the coming of our Lord. Read I John 3:2. John emphasized the appearance of the Lord Jesus Christ.

Of course, one of the greatest portions in the Word of God on the coming of Christ is found in the book of Revelation. Here we are repeatedly told that He is coming again. Read Revelation 19:11-16.

It is very strange that some men will declare that they believe in Jesus Christ and in His first coming but in the same breath deny the Word of God and the prophecies of His return.

III. THE PROPHECIES OF FUTURE EVENTS

Again, we come to some lights on the highway of prophecy. What is out ahead of us?

First, when Christ comes and the saints are snatched away from this earth, the Great Tribulation will take place. Jesus said of this time, "For then shall be great tribulation, such as was not since the beginning of the world to this time, no, nor ever shall be" (Matt. 24:21).

The Great Tribulation is described in the book of Revelation. Woes and judgments are sent upon the world.

Second, the prophecy of the judgment seat of Christ. Christians are going to be judged.

"For we must all appear before the judgment seat of Christ; that every one may receive the things done in his body, according to that he hath done, whether it be good or bad."—II Cor. 5:10.

"But why dost thou judge thy brother? or why dost thou set at nought thy brother? for we shall all stand before the judgment seat of Christ."—Rom. 14:10.

After the judgment seat of Christ and the marriage supper of the Lamb (Rev. 19:7-10), we are coming with our Lord down to this earth, into this atmosphere, when He returns for the Battle of Armageddon. Many portions of Scripture speak of this dread event, but it is enough to see the picture in Revelation 19:17-20. After the Battle of Armageddon will come the judgment of living nations (Matt. 25:31-46).

Next will come the Golden Age—the thousand-year reign of Christ on the earth. In Revelation 20 the "thousand years" is mentioned again and again.

Following this thousand years will come the second resurrection, when the dead, small and great, stand before God, are judged, then sentenced to the lake of fire.

Last, the Word of God speaks of the new heavens and the new earth, wherein dwelleth righteousness.

"Looking for and hasting unto the coming of the day of God, wherein the heavens being on fire shall be dissolved, and the elements shall melt with fervent heat? Nevertheless we, according to his promise, look for new heavens and a new earth, wherein dwelleth righteousness."— II Pet. 3:12,13.

We are facing the new heavens and the new earth.

Do you know Christ as your Saviour? Are you resting in Him? Believe in Him, trust Him, and follow Him.

17 Is He Lord of All?

"For the Son of man is Lord even of the sabbath day."—Matt. 12:8.

To the Pharisees, our Saviour was indeed a revolutionary person. In their eyes He broke all their laws, transgressed their sacred ideals and walked contrary to the precepts of God. Some of the Pharisees were doubtless sincere, but many were hypocritical. Our Lord spoke severe words to the Pharisees and condemned their hypocrisy (Matt. 23).

In the passage before us is the account of our Saviour dealing with the Pharisees. Passing through a field of grain on the Sabbath day, His disciples, being hungry, began to pluck the ears of corn and to eat. When the Pharisees saw it, they said to the Lord, "Behold, thy disciples do that which is not lawful to do upon the sabbath day."

Christ made answer to the Pharisees, "Have ye not read what David did, when he was an hungred, and they that were with him; How he entered into the house of God, and did eat the shewbread, which was not lawful for him to eat, neither for them which were with him, but only for the priests?"

Again He said, "Or have ye not read in the law, how that on the sabbath days the priests in the temple profane the sabbath, and are blameless?"

Then the Lord speaks of Himself: ". . . in this place is one greater than the temple."

The Lord is greater than laws and greater than all.

Now we come to the text, "For the Son of man is Lord even of the sabbath day." Let us see what this portion has to say to us.

I. CHRIST IS LORD OF ALL DAYS

Make Him the Lord of all your days. There should be no vacations from God, no turning from His side, no divorce from pure and holy living. Your desire should be to walk and to talk with Him each day.

Enoch walked with God. This means that day by day Enoch was in the company of God. He rejoiced in the divine presence of our Lord. He desired nothing more than to be in holy communion with God. Surely this should be the desire of every one of us; yet how far we get away from Him, and how little we seem to care for Him!

My friend, He is to be the Lord of all days.

Second, He is to be the Lord of the Lord's Day. We are not entering into a discussion of the change from the observance of the Sabbath day to our keeping of the Lord's Day. It was by the Son of God that God made the world and by Him instituted the Sabbath. It was by the Son that He gave the Ten Commandments on Mt. Sinai and Christ, the Lord of the Sabbath, was authorized to make the alteration from the seventh day to the first day of the week. He arose from the dead, triumphed over the grave; and the Lord's Day is our day of worship, the day on which we remember Him and all He has done for us.

It was on the first day of the week that Jesus appeared to Mary. "Now when Jesus was risen early the first day of the week, he appeared first to Mary Magdalene, out of whom he had cast seven devils."

It was on the first day of the week that He appeared to the two on the road to Emmaus (Luke 24:13-15).

It was on the first day of the week that He appeared to the disciples: "Then the same day at evening, being the first day of the week, when the doors were shut where the disciples were assembled for fear of the Jews, came Jesus and stood in the midst, and saith unto them, Peace be unto you" (John 20:19).

Yes, it was on the first day of the week that Paul preached. We find given in Acts 20:7, "And upon the first day of the week, when the disciples came together to break bread, Paul preached unto them, ready to depart on the morrow; and continued his speech until midnight."

It is upon the first day of the week that we are exhorted to come together and bring our offerings to the Lord. Let us read it in I Corinthians 16:2, "Upon the first day of the week let every one of you lay by him in store, as God hath prospered him, that there be no gatherings when I come."

These are just a few of the portions which can be given from the Word of God to show that Christ is Lord of the Lord's Day. This day belongs to Him. It is not our day, but His day, a day for definite worship and for adoration of the Son of God.

It is not a day to use selfishly, not a day for secular labors, not a day for vacations, not a day for the relaxing of moral standards, not a day for the indulgence of laziness. It is the Lord's Day! Declare now and forever that on this day He shall have the first place.

Third, as we think of Christ, the Lord of days, we must remember that He will be the Lord of our eternal day. There is coming a time when night shall be gone and day will be eternal. We will be under His rule and leadership. We will be with Him throughout the thousand-year reign, then with Him through eternity. He will be the Lord of lords, the King of kings.

Begin now to let Him have His way with you. Recognize that He is the Lord of days. Not *one* day but *all* days belong to Him. Give Him your best!

II. MAKE HIM LORD OF POSSESSIONS

We continue to follow the order in which we have already given some points about our Lord.

First, He is to be the Lord of all possessions. All that you have belongs to Him. Your desire should be to let Him have His way with all that comes into your hands. The Bible requires of us faithfulness.

We find Paul saying to the church in Corinth, "Moreover it is required in stewards, that a man be found faithful" (I Cor. 4:2). Whatever you have is by the goodness of God. He is Lord of all possessions. Remember to ask yourself, "Lord, what wilt thou have me to do?" regarding all things.

Second, He is the Lord of the tithe. We repeat: All things belong to God, but in a peculiar sense, the tithe is the Lord's. No person can use the tithe without suffering. God has spoken very plainly about this.

"Bring ye all the tithes into the storehouse, that there may be meat in mine house, and prove me now herewith, saith the Lord of hosts, if I will not open you the windows of heaven, and pour you out a blessing, that there shall not be room enough to receive it. And I will rebuke the devourer for your sakes, and he shall not destroy the fruits of your ground; neither shall your vine cast her fruit before the time in the field, saith the Lord of hosts."—Mal. 3:10,11.

Our Lord gave His commendation of the tithe when He said to the Pharisees in Matthew 23:23, "Woe unto you, scribes and Pharisees, hypocrites! for ye pay tithe of mint and anise and cummin, and have omitted the weightier matters of the law, judgment, mercy, and faith: these ought ye to have done, and not to leave the other undone."

The tithe is not yours but God's. The blessings of God are promised to those who honor the Lord with the tithe. The windows are opened, and divine spiritual blessings will be yours—blessings that cannot be obtained unless you tithe.

The man who does not tithe is robbing himself and hindering God from doing what the Father wants to do. Time would not permit me to give my testimony on the matter of tithing. I began keeping the scriptural command on the tithe some thirty years ago; and through all of these days, God has abundantly blessed. He has supplied every need; yea, He has gone beyond and given more than I need. When I give that simple testimony, I am cognizant that hundreds in this audience could do the same thing.

But some of you have not started to tithe; or perhaps you tithed for awhile, then turned away from this holy practice. My friend, you are robbing yourself and, worst of all, robbing God.

I repeat: the tithe is not yours but the Lord's. Give Him what belongs to Him. Make Him the Lord of all possessions.

III. MAKE HIM LORD OF PLANS

The one without plans for the future is only half a person. The one who makes plans without considering God is more than a fool.

When we make plans, we are to be quite sure that our Father is in the very center of them all. Listen to what James has to say on this:

"Go to now, ye that say, To day or to morrow we will go into such a city, and continue there a year, and buy and sell, and get gain: Whereas ye know not what shall be on the morrow. For what is your life? It is even a vapour, that appeareth for a little time, and then vanisheth away. For that ye ought to say, If the Lord will, we shall live, and do this, or that."—James 4:13-15.

We are to make plans, but we are to say, "If the Lord will," or, "God willing." The one who makes no plans, who gives no consideration to God, is a fool.

Make your plans and keep Christ in the center.

If your plans touch the financial and the material, be sure Christ is foremost. Be fair and square. Be honest, and God will give His blessings. Keep Him first in time, in talents, in tithe.

If your plans are in the spiritual field, put Him first, or failure is inevitable.

Russell Conwell, the great preacher of Philadelphia, began his work in the First Baptist Church of Minneapolis. He started the Y.M.C.A. in that city. He originated the *North Star* which later became *The Tribune.*

After some time, Russell Conwell was called to a church in Philadelphia. That church worshiped in an old rickety house. Later when he started tearing it down, the neighbors asked, "What are you going to do?" He said, "Build a beautiful one."

After the church was built, he thought of a home for old people who needed a place of refuge. He created that. Then he began Temple University which today has an enrollment of thousands. When death claimed him in his late seventies, it caught him in the midst of plans for the future.

Conwell made his plans but kept God in first place.

You and I are going to fail unless God is in the center of every plan and unless He has the preeminence in every affair.

Let me emphasize: We know not what may come on tomorrow. This behooves us to do everything with a consciousness of the uncertainty of life.

Today I read a strange story which comes from Memphis, Tennessee. A passerby noticed Miss Louise Lohmeyer crouched at the base of a steep embankment, waving weakly with one hand. This account said:

> The other hand clutched the base of a willow sapling whose sharp point had driven into her throat, fracturing her jaw and the base of her skull. She had been hunched there, unable to move or call for help for nearly three hours. Traffic roared by on a busy street just a few yards away.

A newspaper account says Miss Lohmeyer was apparently gathering willow cuttings to plant in her lawn when suddenly she fell upon the willow shaft. She is now at the hospital in critical condition.

I repeat: We do not know what may come on tomorrow; therefore:

Let all plans be laid in and before Him.

Let all plans be in accord with His divine will.

Let all plans be in accord with the transitory nature of this life.

Let all plans be laid with your heart set on souls of men at home and around the world.

May I summarize this message: First, make Christ the Lord of all your days; second, make Him the Lord of possessions; third, make Him the Lord of your plans, the very center of your life.

If He has not been that, then now is the time for a good beginning. Say it now, "From this moment on, Christ shall be Lord of my life—the Lord of every day, of every plan, and of all possessions."

18 Have You Forgotten?

"And they remembered his words."—Luke 24:8.

Forgetfulness robs us of many blessings. There are words we should remember, acts we should recall. Remembering these things will bring joy and encouragement.

Some experiences need to be forgotten. For example, our honest failures—when we have done our best but still failed. Such experiences should be put behind us. Don't waste time lamenting honest failures. However, let it be remembered that such failures can prove good for us. These failures can teach us what and what not to do.

Now, what should we remember?

I. REMEMBER THE DAY OF SALVATION

Don't get far away from the experience of regeneration. Remember the day when God spoke peace to your heart. Remember that day when you saw yourself a lost sinner and Christ as the only Saviour and you accepted Him.

The Apostle Paul never forgot. He grew in grace and in the knowledge of the Lord, but he never grew away from the experience which he had with Christ on the road to Damascus. After years of preaching, he still repeated the story of redeeming grace.

We find him before King Agrippa, telling of his conversion. The words were simple but Spirit-filled. We do not wonder that Agrippa said, "Almost thou persuadest me to be a Christian." With great intensity, the Apostle Paul said, "I would to God, that not only thou, but also all that hear me this day, were both almost, and altogether such as I am, except these bonds."

Never get far away from the experience of salvation. Each day return in your thinking to the time when Jesus spoke peace to your heart.

This week a man came to see me. He was saved last Sunday. He came to tell me of his great joy in Jesus Christ. May he never forget what the Lord did for him!

Our experience of salvation should be new, vibrant and all-consuming. Every time we pray, we should be brought face to face with the fact that we have been made the children of God through faith in Jesus Christ. Every time we come before the Lord pleading forgiveness for our misdeeds, we should remember that we can do so only because we are His children, and we can claim the promise of I John 1:9.

Remember your salvation!

II. REMEMBER THE DAY OF YOUR PROMISES TO GOD

I have no time to waste with any person who has never made promises to the Lord. There are some supercilious, superficial, shallow-brained individuals who say they never make promises to anybody, including God. Shame on you!

I want to take you back to the time when you made some promises to the Lord.

First, you promised to be faithful. That promise was all-inclusive. You meant to be faithful in the reading of His Word, in prayer, in church attendance—in all Christian activity. God understood the meaning of your heart when you made that promise. He knew the weakness of the flesh, but He stood ready to give you aid.

Have you been faithful? Have you remembered your promise to God?

Second, you promised to be honest with the Lord. I speak now of giving. I have never known a great Christian who was dishonest in money matters. Be honest in tithing, and God will pour out His blessings upon you.

"Bring ye all the tithes into the storehouse, that there may be meat in mine house, and prove me now herewith, saith the Lord of hosts, if I will not open you the windows of heaven, and pour you out a blessing, that there shall not be room enough to receive it."—Mal. 3:10.

Third, you promised to be a witness. You believed in the importance of witnessing; you received His command to go and to tell others about Him—but have you done it? Have you been faithful in witnessing for your Saviour?

Yes, remember your promises, your solemn promises, your deep promises, your meaningful promises! Have you been true to the promises you made to the Lord? Let your memory be stirred, your mind activated. Renew these promises and do what you promised the Lord to do.

Perhaps a promise was made at the death of your little one. To me there is nothing so sad as the death of a baby or a small child. I have watched the tears of mothers and fathers. But I wonder if they will do what, in the hour of sadness, they felt impressed to do.

Perhaps a promise was made at the illness of a loved one. During the sickness you promised God that certain things would be done: you would be faithful in church attendance, honest in tithing, true in witnessing—but have you fulfilled those promises? Perhaps you told the Lord that, if He would heal your loved one, you would do certain things for Him which you have not done.

Perhaps in the time of your own illness you turned to the Lord and promised, if His healing hand would be placed upon you, you would devote the rest of your life in faithful service to Him.

I have listened to ten thousand promises such as these, but I have seen very few of them fulfilled. I have watched people come out of hospitals and turn away from God. I have seen them become destitute of the blessings of God.

I beg of you, heed carefully this admonition. Remember your promises to the Lord!

Perhaps your promise was made in the day of financial reverses. Everything had been swept away. You wondered if anything more could be done. But in that time God was faithful and delivered you from difficulty. I now call upon you to remember what God did in your behalf. I remind you of all the promises you made to the Lord. Now fulfill these promises. Return to them and begin anew to give your wholehearted service to God.

III. REMEMBER THE DAY WHEN SIN MARRED YOUR LIFE

What I am suggesting now is not pleasant, yet it is necessary. Ordinarily we tell people to forget their sins and turn from their evil ways. But, for the sake of this message, I want you to remember when sin marred your life so you can heed it more.

It is doubtful that Abraham ever forgot when he lied about himself and his wife. Abraham, the friend of God, the father of the faithful, such a good and righteous man, yet he sinned.

It is doubtful that Jacob could ever forget his sin. He was forgiven and greatly used of God, but his memory doubtless clung to his evil.

It is doubtful that David ever forgot the awfulness of his sin. Though forgiveness was given him, the marks of sin were still there. He did not forget though God had forgiven him.

What are the sins that mar and scar?

First, the sins of the world—following after the evil of this sinful day—mar and scar. Great care must be exercised by young and old that we are not engulfed in the lawful, damnable, dirty sins of this day.

Second, the sins of indifference. What scars these sins make upon us! Pray that God will make you sensitive to evil. Pray that you may not become an indifferent person. Pray that your heart will keep tender toward the things of God.

Third, the sins of evil speaking. Let your language be clear, clean and pure. Do people know that you are a child of God by the way you speak?

There are many other sins that mar and scar. If Christ has forgiven you, then rejoice and let God have His full and righteous way.

Would you let me suggest what to do about sin? First, turn from it. With resolute determination, turn from sin. Second, hate sin with all of your being. Refuse to cling to it. Third, denounce it. Let your whole soul be turned against it, but also denounce it with your lips.

Fourth, help others to turn from sin. By encouraging someone else in the right path, you will be stronger.

Remember the day when sin marred your life. Remember the awfulness of evil. Remember how God hates sin. Pray that you may have the same attitude toward that which is wrong.

IV. REMEMBER THE DAY OF YOUR DEDICATION

Every child of God should have a definite time of giving all to Christ, one definite dedication and other rededications as the Spirit leads.

First, there should be a dedication of your all to Christ when you are saved. Shame, shame upon some who get saved and refuse to give everything to the Lord!

However, your complete dedication may be at a later time. Your understanding of spiritual matters will be greater as you read the Word of God and pray. Therefore, that time of definite dedication may come after you are already saved.

The failure to make a dedication of your all to Christ may be the fault of the pastor or the evangelist or the Christian worker who helps you. Therefore, be sure that you understand that every Christian should give himself completely to the Lord.

If you have never dedicated your all to Him, then do it now. Let this be the moment when you say, "Dear Lord, take me."

> Take my life, and let it be
> Consecrated, Lord, to Thee;
> Take my hands, and let them move
> At the impulse of Thy love.
>
> Take my feet, and let them be
> Swift and beautiful for Thee;
> Take my voice, and let me sing,
> Always, only for my King.
>
> Take my silver and my gold,
> Not a mite would I withhold;
> Take my moments and my days,
> Let them flow in ceaseless praise.

Take my will, and make it Thine,
It shall be no longer mine;
Take my heart, it is Thine own;
It shall be Thy royal throne.

Lord, I give my life to Thee,
Thine forevermore to be;
Lord, I give my life to Thee,
Thine forevermore to be.

Last, if you have dedicated your all to Christ, then remember this act of dedication. Are you being true to your Saviour? Are you staying by the promises made to Him?

Joshua made many promises to the Lord. He led the people of Israel as a valiant soldier, but the time that impresses me most is when Joshua came to the close of his life. We find him standing with the people of Israel and hearing these words from his lips: "But as for me and my house, we will serve the Lord." Joshua was over one hundred years old when these words were spoken. He had fought long and valiantly. He had obeyed the commands of the Lord. Now, as he reached the end of the way, he could say, "As for me and my house, we will serve the Lord." This was complete and final dedication for the old saint of God.

Yes, my friend, remember the day of your salvation. Remember the promises you made to God. Remember when sin marred your life. Remember the day of your dedication to God.

May these words be used by the Spirit of God to draw you near to the side of the Saviour. Let the words of our Lord strike upon your ears, even as the words of the two angels struck upon the ears of the disciples when they came to the sepulcher on the first day of the week. When the angel spoke to them, they remembered His words.

I hope you will say in this hour, "My Lord has spoken to me. I have been turning away from His words and His commands. From this moment on I give myself in full surrender to my blessed Christ."

19 The Silliness of the Sinful and Selfish

"Then the Pharisees went out, and held a council against him, how they might destroy him."—Matt. 12:14.

The Bible is full of the accounts of the foolishness of men and tells us of these failures for our encouragement, our warning, our edification.

We are told about the failure of Noah. This man had been blessed of God, yet he drank wine and in his drunk state was uncovered within his tent.

We read about the foolishness of Abraham. This great man, the father of the faithful, the man whose name stands high in God's Honor Roll, did a foolish thing when he tried to pass off his wife as his sister. Only because of the plagues upon Pharaoh was the truth brought out.

Moses, one of the greatest this world has ever known, also performed a foolish act when, in a fit of anger, he spoke out against the rock where God had promised water and smote it twice (Num. 20).

Samson, chosen judge of the people of Israel, did foolishly when he turned away from God and began to run with the heathen.

David, the man after God's own heart, was foolish when he looked upon Bath-sheba and brought upon his head judgment because of his sin.

Now the question: Why does the Bible give these accounts about the foolishness of men? That we might hate and avoid sin. The Bible does not encourage us to do evil; it encourages us to do right.

The accounts of the failures of others are given to turn us from evil and lead us to the Lord.

In Matthew 12 is the interesting story of our Master going into the synagogue.

When a man with a withered hand came before Him, the people said, "Is it lawful to heal on the sabbath days?" They asked this question so they might accuse Him.

The Lord made answer: "What man shall there be among you, that shall have one sheep, and if it fall into a pit on the sabbath day, will he not lay hold on it, and lift it out? How much then is a man better than a sheep? Wherefore it is lawful to do well on the sabbath days."

Then Jesus said to the man, "Stretch forth thine hand." He stretched it forth, and it was restored whole like the other.

Now, we find the text for this message: "Then the Pharisees went out, and held a council against him, how they might destroy him." The Pharisees were sinful and selfish, and they behaved foolishly. Let me give my reasons:

I. CHRIST CANNOT BE DESTROYED

Baal can be destroyed. The idol of Nebuchadnezzar can turn to dust. But Christ lives on.

The Lord is our ever-living Saviour. He was with God in the beginning, and He is with God at this time. The changes and fluctuations of this world do not change the fact that Christ is the same yesterday, today and forever.

He was not destroyed by evil men in His day. There was a time when they sought to cast Jesus over a cliff, but the Master walked through their midst and escaped their sinful hands.

On the cross of Calvary they thought they had destroyed Jesus. The crowd stood around and mocked—laughed at Him—ridiculed Him—but remember, He was not destroyed by evil men.

And Christ cannot be destroyed by evil men today. There are those who would seek to tear Him down, to take away His glory. They want to make Him just an ordinary man. But Christ is the Son of God. All of the vain words of Bob Ingersoll, Clarence Darrow or

Voltaire cannot take away one particle of the glory from the Son of God. He could not be destroyed. He cannot be destroyed.

Let us remember our Christ lives forever. He is the same forever. He was with God in the beginning. He will be with God throughout all the endless ages of eternity.

If I were to see a small lad five or six years of age standing on the side of Lookout Mountain and shovelling away at the dirt, the rocks and the stones with a teaspoon, I would know he would have a better chance of one day eradicating the mountain than all men would have at destroying Jesus.

The Pharisees, like foolish men, sought a way whereby they could destroy Him: How silly was this act!

Ignoring the Bible cannot destroy it. Men may fail to read this Word, they may not know what it says, but here it is; and our ignorance does not take it from our presence. It is only natural that men should hate the Word. This Bible condemns their sin. This Book reveals coming judgments. This Book tells of the punishment which will be brought upon them who deny the Son of God.

You have in your possession a Book which is eternal. So study it. Rejoice in it. It is God's eternal Word to you.

II. THE ETERNAL PURPOSE OF CHRIST
CANNOT BE DESTROYED

The purpose of God marches on, even as daylight follows dark. Nothing can stay the purpose of the Son of God. What is it?

First, it is to bring men to Himself. Christ came into this world and died upon the cross and rose again that men might be saved. The way of salvation has been made so plain, so clear, that no one need err. All can know and be saved. It is the purpose of God to save and to bring men to Himself that they might abide in His presence forever.

Again, His purpose is to establish a perfect world—a world without sin. In this He shall not fail. The perfection of the first world before sin entered in shall be reached again. Our Christ is coming! We are going to be received into His presence. We are going to reign with Him a thousand years upon this earth. After the thousand years, there will be a brief uprising of old Satan; then the Devil will be cast into the lake of fire and brimstone. The things which we now see will be dissolved and taken away. There will come the new heavens and the new earth wherein dwelleth righteousness (II Pet. 3:13).

Let your mind and heart lay hold upon the great things of God. Do not be short in seeing what our blessed Lord has for you. We are the children of God, and one day we shall be in the presence of our Saviour.

Finally, the eternal purpose of Christ is that all sin and suffering, sorrow and death shall be taken away.

"And God shall wipe away all tears from their eyes; and there shall be no more death, neither sorrow, nor crying, neither shall there be any more pain: for the former things are passed away."—Rev. 21:4.

The tabernacle of God is going to be with men. We are going to dwell with Him and be His people, and God will be with us. In that matchless, wonderful day, all sorrow, all heartache will be no more. The disappointments, the failures will be done away; and we shall be with Him forevermore!

 **Inside or Outside**

"Woe unto you, scribes and Pharisees, hypocrites! for ye make clean the outside of the cup and of the platter, but within they are full of extortion and excess.

"Thou blind Pharisee, cleanse first that which is within the cup and platter, that the outside of them may be clean also.

"Woe unto you, scribes and Pharisees, hypocrites! for ye are like unto whited sepulchres, which indeed appear beautiful outward, but are within full of dead men's bones, and of all uncleanness.

"Even so ye also outwardly appear righteous unto men, but within ye are full of hypocrisy and iniquity."—Matt. 23:25-28.

"And he said, That which cometh out of the man, that defileth the man.

"For from within, out of the heart of men, proceed evil thoughts, adulteries, fornications, murders,

"Thefts, covetousness, wickedness, deceit, lasciviousness, an evil eye, blasphemy, pride, foolishiness:

"All these evil things come from within, and defile the man."—Mark 7:20-23.

"For, when we were come into Macedonia, our flesh had no rest, but we were troubled on every side; without were fightings, within were fears."—II Cor. 7:5.

The late Hyman Appelman said from this pulpit, "No great nation has ever fallen from the outside." This same statement was repeated in his book, *Formula for Revival.* The entire paragraph in which this sentence is found reads:

> There comes last the period of deterioration and destruction. No great nation has ever fallen from the outside. Neither Egypt, nor Assyria, nor Persia, nor Greece, nor Rome, nor Spain, nor France, nor Italy fell, as history plainly records, under the onslaught of enemies from the outside. It has always been the faults, the failures, the corruptions, the rottenness on the inside that has cracked up a people.
>
> Right now our own country is standing with one foot in the period of leisure and luxury, while the other foot is balanced precariously over the frightening abyss of deterioration and destruction.

A contemplation of this truth, "No great nation has ever fallen from the outside," will make us see that corruption, defeat and disintegration begin on the inside.

How plainly the Lord Jesus emphasized the inner need of man! When He spoke to the Pharisees, it was to condemn their inner corruption. Christ said, "For from within, out of the hearts of men proceed evil thoughts, adulteries, etc."

The Apostle Paul knew also that it is from within that one must be strong. Trouble and fighting may come from without, but from within come fears.

Now, let us think upon this subject for a moment.

I. CONSIDER THE FALL OF NATIONS

The history of nations reveals that weakness which leads to fall begins within. The failure of a people can always be traced to inner sin and corruption.

Strong nations do not war against strong nations. But strong nations encroach upon weak nations, made weak by inner corruption.

Israel always fell in moments of inner weakness. When Israel was strong, nations turned away from her; but in her hour of weakness, they encroached upon her and sapped away her strength.

When Nebuchadnezzar came against Judah, Judah was weak because of inner dissension and sin.

Likewise, Babylon fell when inner corruption weakened her.

The same applies to Egypt, Greece and Rome.

Nations fall from within, not from the outside. This is something that our own nation should consider earnestly and thoughtfully. The power of this country will be found in inner integrity and holiness. The weakness will likewise be found in our sinfulness, our despising of God's laws, our refusal to do that which is right.

Nations fall from within. No nation can rise and blame her fall upon another. A nation's destruction begins with her own weakness.

II. THE FALL OF CHRISTIAN INSTITUTIONS

Let us give consideration to the Christian home. Is the home weakened from the inside or from the outside? Does it begin to fall because of inner failure or outward power? Every person's answer will be, "The home fails when weakness takes hold of the inside." Outside influences have a part in the destruction of a home, but the disintegration begins within.

Christian homes are made strong by very simple methods. First, a love for God and a determination that He have the first place. Second, a delight in the Bible and in prayer must not be forgotten in the building of a Christian home. Third, a love for righteousness and a hatred for evil.

It was Joshua who said, "As for me and my house, we will serve the Lord." Such determination will mean the standing of a home. Such a decision will be a bulwark against all destructive forces.

Colleges and universities, as well as other institutions founded in the name of Christ, have always fallen from the inside. In the early days of this nation, all colleges had religious backgrounds; then they turned away from them. The failure: Inside!

No college will stand unless there is an inner determination to put God first. No home will continue unless from within there is a solemn determination that God will rule the household.

III. THE FALL OF INDIVIDUALS

All failure begins within.

Simon Peter denied his Lord because of inner weakness.

When we are strong within, outside opposition will serve to

strengthen us. When we are right within our hearts, then outside opposition will sweeten us. When we are right, outside opposition will stimulate us.

Now we come to the crux of the entire matter. What are the inner sins that we can destroy? And what are the ways whereby the Christian can be made strong?

First, consider the sins that weaken and destroy—immorality—impure living; the sins of dishonesty—unjust thinking; the sins of jealousy—a wrong balance toward others; the sins of selfishness—wrong desires about earthly things; the sins of low aim and indifference toward the highest and best. These are the inside sins that weaken and destroy.

How vividly this is illustrated to my own mind by two lieutenants of the Air Force who rode with me from Fort Worth to Dallas in the airport limousine this morning. Both men had been up all night. They had spent the hours in drunkenness and sin. All they could do was talk about their sin in lurid and dirty detail.

The entire scene was sickening and disgusting. These boys were destroying themselves. They failed to see that it is righteousness that gives peace, happiness and purpose in life. They were following a low aim which could do nothing but destroy them.

What are the attributes of a strong life?

First, Bible study. The Word of God must speak to our hearts. Someone has written:

> The Bible is a light and guide,
> Ever near the Christian's side;
> A source of comfort and of power,
> Part of our Heavenly Father's dower.
>
> The Bible is a weapon of offense
> In life's great battle, so intense;
> It is the mighty Spirit's sword
> To overcome the Devil's horde.
>
> The entrance of the Word giveth light
> And illuminates the darkest night;
> The Word is a lamp unto our feet,
> To keep us on the Jesus Street.

This Flashlight is ready for you,
To help you always in all you do;
Then why not use it every day
To guide you in the Heavenly way?

The Bible is a light and guide,
Ever near the Christian's side;
Then why not read it more and more
And claim the blessings there in store?

Second, prayer. Pray about everything. Failure to pray will be the beginning of weakness and destruction. "Pray without ceasing" must be our constant motto. No one can pray too much. Most of us are guilty of praying too little.

Third, meditation. Think upon your way. Seek to orient yourself to the teachings of the Bible. Carefully meditate upon what God says.

Fourth, helping others. Jesus went about doing good. He was constantly occupied with assisting someone else. He lived for others. He delighted in helping the needy. He had an eye for the blind and an ear to hear the cry of the desolate.

Fifth, being filled with the Holy Spirit. This should certainly have first place, but I have saved it for a concluding point. To be what God wants us to be, we must be filled with the Holy Spirit. It is by the filling of the Holy Spirit that we are made inwardly strong and outwardly ready for God's work.

Is this for any special person or any small group? No! The filling of the Holy Spirit is for every Christian. Failure to be filled with the Spirit of God usually results from two things: a lack of emptiness of self and sin and an unwillingness to let God have His way.

No person is going to be filled with the Spirit who is unwilling to give up the sinful things of this world. They may be ever so small and insignificant as far as the world is concerned but big in the sight of God.

No person will be filled with the Spirit unless he is willing for God to use and guide him.

God is waiting to give this blessing to His children. He wants you to be filled, empowered and ready for service. Then why will you go on in weakness and ineffective service? The answer can only be that you love sin and refuse to turn from it, or that you do not want to do His holy will.

Where does individual failure begin? Within the individual heart. Turn loose and let God have His way. Outside difficulties are as nothing when the Holy Spirit has His way within. Successful living, inner peace, outward usefulness—all can be yours when you give way to the Holy Spirit.

Your difficulties do not arise from the situations around you but from your own heart. Child of God, make a full and determined surrender of yourself to God.

And now a word to the unsaved ones: My friend, you are on the way that leads to destruction, not on the way that leads to life everlasting. Jesus said, "I am the way." Without Christ, your road can only lead to destruction, endless night and Hell. The only hope for you is to receive Christ as your Saviour.

21 Men Who Believe

"And he said, Lord, I believe. And he worshipped him."—John 9:38.

"For the which cause I also suffer these things: nevertheless I am not ashamed: for I know whom I have believed, and am persuaded that he is able to keep that which I have committed unto him against that day."—II Tim. 1:12.

A few days ago in my reading, I came across three outstanding words at the conclusion of a paragraph—"men who believe." Here is the entire paragraph, written about Charles Haddon Spurgeon of England a few weeks after his death.

> He believed. Everything was a reality. When he was in his study, when he went into the pulpit—everything was a reality. He stood as God's representative to man and as man's representative to God. The man who believes every word he says is a power. God works sometimes through narrow-minded men, sometimes through weak men, but always through men who believe.

That gives the secret of the great ministry of Spurgeon, a man who believed.

It should be written about all of us who name the name of Christ. The Bible should be real to us. We should believe every word. Its truth must be food for our souls, refreshment when we are tired, encouragement when we are discouraged.

Our salvation must be precious. We must know that we are saved, that we have been born again by the power of God.

A blind man who had received his sight at the hands of Jesus said, "Lord, I believe." The miracle of his restoration might have been a mystery to him, but he knew the One who had worked the miracle.

Our call to His service must be vital; the freshness of the first day that God called us must be real.

On last evening a young man came up to me at the close of the service in Winston-Salem and said, "God called me to preach a number of years ago, but I turned away. Last night your message spoke to my heart, and I am determined to do God's will."

The call of God was upon him through his years of delay, but the vitality of the call had escaped him. He was not doing what God wanted him to do.

Now, let us think about men who believe.

I. MEN WHO BELIEVE HAVE BEEN SAVED BY POWER DIVINE

All men greatly used of God have had sacred experiences. The first and foremost experience is salvation, and this vital and holy experience must never leave us.

Did Peter forget the day Christ saved him? He was brought to the Lord by his own brother, Andrew. The preciousness of his entrance into the family of God through faith in Jesus Christ never left him.

Did the Apostle Paul forget that momentous day when Christ became his Saviour? Did he forget the voice that spoke from Heaven unto him? Paul did not forget; he repeated his experience many times.

Did John forget that day Christ came into his heart? No. The son of thunder became the apostle of love.

My friend, forget not the day Christ became your Saviour. Don't allow anything to dull the memory of that sacred time when you accepted Christ as Saviour and made Him Lord and Master of your life.

Some of you may testify that you were saved out of a life of great sin. For you, the experience of coming to Jesus was revolutionary.

I was reading about a little family who lived in a plain shack.

The father spent all his money on drink, while the wife and children suffered for the necessities of life.

Finally the father decided to break up his home and send the children to an institution.

A good Christian saw the children of this poor family sitting on the front steps of their home Sunday after Sunday. One day he went in to invite them to church and Sunday school. When he met the father, this Christian told him how he too had once been a drunkard. He told about how he had spent all his money in sin, then how God had saved him, changed his life and given him a happy home.

That night the sinful man said to his wife, "I love you and the children, but when this awful appetite comes upon me, I simply must have a drink. If it took the clothes off my back, if it killed me, I would be forced to have a drink.

"But God heard this man's prayer and saved him. Maybe he will save me, too." He and his wife fell on their knees and prayed, "Lord, be merciful to me a sinner and save me for Jesus' sake." God heard the prayer and saved the man and his wife. Today the entire family has a happy home, and they are serving Christ.

Some of you may have had a like experience. Your life was evil and destitute until Christ took over. But again there may be some of you who do not have such a vivid recollection of your salvation.

You might be like the great F. B. Meyer. Dr. Meyer was noted in England and America for his Bible teaching. He said the following:

> I suppose that for me, the new birth was like the dawn of the morning. I never had any marked experience that I can look back upon.
>
> When I was about fourteen years of age, a new minister came to our church and insisted very much on the necessity of the new birth. I was then troubled because I could not point to any time or place or cause.
>
> Then it was that I went to hear Mr. Spurgeon and heard him say that a man might not know his birthdate but be quite sure that he was living. That helped me, for I did not know my spiritual birthday, but I knew I was alive.

The great essential is for you to know that Christ is yours, and that all is well. If you are saved, give your testimony for Christ and let others see and know that you believe.

II. MEN WHO BELIEVE ARE GOOD ADVERTISE-MENTS FOR CHRIST

J. Hudson Taylor, the pioneer missionary to China and the founder of the China Inland Mission, was a good advertisement for Christ. He came to the Lord Jesus, received Him as Saviour, then drew every day upon the fathomless wealth of Christ.

Hudson Taylor doubtless had many secrets of going on with God, but there was one simple, profound secret of drawing upon the Saviour for every need of his life.

Is this not a word for us? We need not only to believe in Jesus Christ, but to draw upon Him for all our needs.

David Livingstone was a good advertisement for Christ. He is said to be one of the world's greatest missionaries. He had a profound faith in God and in Christ. He relied upon the Lord for every need.

George Mueller was a good advertisement for Christ. He was one who believed, and his belief led him to a simple faith in the Son of God. He believed that Christ could and would supply every need of his life and work.

But every Christian should be a good advertisement for Jesus. Every Christian! Every Christian's testimony for Christ should be strong. Let others know that you are drinking at the fountain and that God is sustaining you.

Now, how can you advertise for your Saviour?

First, let others know He is your Saviour by speaking for Him. Testify of His grace. Tell of His mercy. Review His acts of love toward you. Tell others about Him. This we are commanded to do.

Second, let others know that He is your Saviour by your consecration. So live that people will see Christ in you and they will be constrained to know that something has happened in your experience which has made you a new creature in Christ Jesus. Plainly and simply, live so that people can know you belong to Christ.

A man opened a restaurant in the old days. Needing someone to help him, he put an advertisement in a paper. One boy came in and applied for the position. The man told him that he would pay $10.00 per week and meals. The boy said, "How good are the meals?" The man patted his big stomach and said, "I eat here." He was a good ad for the restaurant.

Are you a good advertisement for our Saviour? Can others look at you and know that Christ is able to give peace, joy and satisfaction? So live that people can see and know that you are a child of God.

Are you constantly advertising for Him?

On one occasion when Fritz Kreisler had several hours to spend between trains in a certain city, he decided to walk around and see the sights. He stopped in front of a music store and saw in the window something that he wanted to purchase. He went into the store and laid his violin case with his name on it, on the counter. When the shopkeeper saw the name on the case, he thought the famous musician's violin had been stolen by the man.

Excusing himself, he went back to his office and called the police. Soon they came in and accused this man of stealing Kreisler's violin. When he insisted he was Kreisler, they would not believe it.

Finally he said to the shopkeeper, "Do you have one of Fritz Kreisler's records in your shop?"

"Yes," replied the man.

"Please play this number for me," said Kreisler, "and then I'll play the same number on my violin."

The record was put on the machine. They listened to the music which had been recorded by Kreisler. Then he picked up his violin and played this same number. The policemen and shopkeeper stood in amazement. They knew now that this was the Fritz Kreisler. The policeman apologized profusely and let him go.

It is one thing to profess that we know Jesus Christ, but it is something else to live so that others can see and know that we are the children of God.

Third, let others know that Christ is your Saviour by your childlike trust and faith in Him. Believe God! Know that He cares for you. Simply rest in His arms and have confidence that He will take care of you and your every need. The Lord Jesus is saying that to us when He says,

"Therefore I say unto you, Take no thought for your life, what ye shall eat, or what ye shall drink; nor yet for your body, what ye shall put on. Is not the life more than meat, and the body than raiment? Behold the fowls of the air: for they sow not, neither do they reap, nor gather into barns; yet your heavenly Father feedeth them. Are ye not much better than they?"—Matt. 6:25, 26.

"Therefore take no thought, saying, What shall we eat? or, What shall we drink? or, Wherewithal shall we be clothed?

"(For after all these things do the Gentiles seek:) for your heavenly Father knoweth that ye have need of all these things.

"But seek ye first the kingdom of God, and his righteousness; and all these things shall be added unto you.

"Take therefore no thought for the morrow: for the morrow shall take thought for the things of itself. Sufficient unto the day is the evil thereof."—Matt. 6:31-34.

I say be a good advertisement for Jesus Christ. Let people know they are in the company of a believer in Christ.

III. MEN WHO BELIEVE HAVE CONFIDENCE IN GOD

What a day it was when Stephen gave his address to the rulers of Israel! He was filled with the Spirit of God and with the message of our Saviour.

With power he testified of Christ. With confidence he told of the work of God in behalf of sinners. The rulers were angry, but that didn't change the fact that God was with Stephen. This humble deacon of the early church in Jerusalem was conscious of the fact that God was with him. He was confident of the presence of God. When the rulers rushed upon him, he saw Jesus standing at the right hand of God. His confidence did not change.

Moses had confidence in God when he came to the Red Sea and led the people to the other side—upon dry land.

When God told Joshua to go around Jericho once each day for seven days, and on the seventh day, seven times—Joshua believed God, that the city would be given into their hands.

When Daniel was told that he must not pray to God, he went

into his chamber, opened the window toward Jerusalem, and poured out his heart to the Lord.

He had confidence in God when he was cast into the den of lions. He knew that God would watch over him.

The need of the hour is men who believe, men who have confidence in God. We are always looking for better methods and better organizations, but God is looking for better men—men of prayer, men of faith, men filled with the Holy Spirit.

Jesus trained twelve men. One was a traitor, but eleven went on to do the job given them. None of them were great in talents or learning; but they were great in holiness, great in faith, great in love, great in fidelity, and great for God. They believed God and rested upon His Word.

Jesus said, "Have faith in God." The men who have shaken this world have had faith in God. They have had confidence to launch out into the deep and to do what God commanded.

You cannot stop a man who believes God is with him. Barriers cannot hold back the person who is set on following the Lord.

When Napoleon's army invaded Russia, they came to a village where everyone had fled except one man. He was a woodsman, with the handle of his ax stuck in his leather belt. When they started to shoot him he showed such calmness and courage that the French captain decided to save his life.

However, the captain said, "We will mark you. We will brand you for life." They heated a branding iron and stamped the letter "N" in the palm of his hand.

"What does that mean?" asked the woodsman.

"The letter 'N' stands for Napoleon. You now belong to our emperor."

The man, always a loyal Russian, thought it was time to show his loyalty. He took the ax from his belt, put his hand on the block and cut that hand off at the wrist, saying, "That hand may belong to Napoleon, but I am a Russian; and if I must die, I die a Russian."

Let us stand for our Saviour whatever the cost.

 # A Warm Hand on a Cold Casket

"Let not your heart be troubled: ye believe in God, believe also in me.

"In my Father's house are many mansions: if it were not so, I would have told you. I go to prepare a place for you.

"And if I go and prepare a place for you, I will come again, and receive you unto myself; that where I am, there ye may be also.

"And whither I go ye know, and the way ye know.

"Thomas saith unto him, Lord, we know not whither thou goest; and how can we know the way?

"Jesus saith unto him, I am the way, the truth, and the life: no man cometh unto the Father, but by me."—John 14:1-6.

"And I saw a new heaven and a new earth: for the first heaven and the first earth were passed away; and there was no more sea.

"And I John saw the holy city, new Jerusalem, coming down from God out of heaven, prepared as a bride adorned for her husband.

"And I heard a great voice out of heaven saying, Behold, the tabernacle of God is with men, and he will dwell with them, and they shall be his people, and God himself shall be with them, and be their God.

"And God shall wipe away all tears from their eyes: and there shall be no more death, neither sorrow, nor crying, neither shall there be any more pain: for the former things are passed away.

"And he that sat upon the throne said, Behold, I make all things new. And he said unto me, Write: for these words are true and faithful."—Rev. 21:1-5.

These Scriptures I read at a recent funeral service. While standing at the graveside, I unconsciously rested my hand on the metal casket and read Psalm 23.

"The Lord is my shepherd; I shall not want.

"He maketh me to lie down in green pastures: he leadeth me beside the still waters.

"He restoreth my soul: he leadeth me in the paths of righteousness for his name's sake.

"Yea, though I walk through the valley of the shadow of death, I will fear no evil: for thou art with me; thy rod and thy staff they comfort me.

"Thou preparest a table before me in the presence of mine enemies: thou anointest my head with oil; my cup runneth over.

"Surely goodness and mercy shall follow me all the days of my life: and I will dwell in the house of the Lord for ever."

When I finished reading this Psalm, I prayed for the comfort of the family. While my hand still rested on the casket, a number of thoughts raced through my mind, thoughts that I expressed partially in my prayer, thoughts that helped me and I trust helped others. I mention them now for our blessing and help. Even as I preach, I can seem to feel my hand upon the cool metal of the casket, the gentle breeze blowing down the hillside at Greenwood Cemetery, the quiet solemnity of the Silent City of the Dead. Here are the thoughts:

I. LIFE IS BRIEF AND UNCERTAIN

At its very best and at its longest, life is still brief. The Bible tells us of the brevity and uncertainty of life. "For what is your life? It is even a vapour, that appeareth for a little time, and then vanisheth away" (James 4:14).

Many verses indicate the frailty of man and the uncertainty of his days. The psalmist says, "He remembered that they were but flesh; a wind that passeth away, and cometh not again" (Ps. 78:39).

Isaiah expressed it in this way: "But we are all as an unclean thing, and all our righteousnesses are as filthy rags; and we all do fade as a leaf; and our iniquities, like the wind, have taken us away" (Isa. 64:6).

In the light of the brevity and uncertainty of life, let us resolve to do three things.

First, do all the good we can while we live. Let every day be filled with good deeds, generous acts, kind thoughts, sympathetic action. This is the kind of life that blesses others, and this kind of influence lives on after death.

Yesterday they had the funeral in Broxton, Georgia, of Aunt Mary Hays. The service was held at the Free Will Baptist Church at 2:00 o'clock. Aunt Mary Hays was a colored woman with a will of iron and a heart of gold. She died at the age of 85, just as her greatest dream was within weeks of realization. They are building near Broxton the Mary Hays Memorial Home for aged Negro men and women. It is almost finished except for the roof and the furnishings. If Aunt Mary had lived until the first of the year, she would have seen the poor, the homeless, the sick carried into the new surroundings.

Aunt Mary was the daughter of slave parents. Throughout her life she had a heart for those in need. She washed, ironed, cooked, chopped wood, picked cotton, and brought up her brothers and sisters and her own children in the love and admonition of the Lord. She was a great believer in prayer and in hard work.

Early in life Aunt Mary showed concern for helpless old people. She was always carrying food to the aged and the bedridden. When she fell and broke her hip, she was so concerned about an aged neighbor that she got on crutches and went about the community, visiting Negroes and whites, trying to raise money to build a little one-room house for the helpless neighbor. She raised some money and got some men to do the work.

That was the real beginning of the Mary Hays Memorial Home; and now, because of the efforts of Aunt Mary Hays, they are completing in a few weeks a $25,000 building to care for helpless old people. The story of Aunt Mary Hays was written up in *The Atlanta Constitution*.

We could solve a lot of problems, relieve a lot of heartaches if just a few were like that old Negro.

Resolve to do all the good you can. Spend yourself and be spent in the Lord's service that others might be blessed. Remember that the greatest good is in witnessing to people about Jesus Christ and getting them ready for eternity.

Second, in considering the brevity of life, turn from all evil. First, turn from sin and evil because God hates sin and He cannot bless you as long as you continue in sin.

Next, not only is evil against God, but evil is against you. It wars against your best interests. The man who engages in sin is his own worst enemy.

Again, turn from evil because your influence will hurt others. Considering the brevity of life, be careful not to give any part of your life and influence to Satan.

Again, life is brief; therefore, take your stand for the right. Send up your flag and let people know what you believe. Respect the man for his convictions even though you may feel he is entirely wrong, but have little regard or respect for the man who refuses to stand for anything.

Again, because of the brevity of life, don't worry or fret, but trust in God. We should often read these verses in Psalm 37:

"Fret not thyself because of evildoers, neither be thou envious against the workers of iniquity. . . . Trust in the Lord, and do good; so shalt thou dwell in the land, and verily thou shalt be fed."

How wonderful they are!

Don't worry about criticism, but have faith in God and let Him answer the critics.

Don't worry about daily needs; know that God will supply.

Put down all fear and rest wholly upon the Lord, committing your ways unto Him and trusting Him. Many of our fears are largely imaginary anyway and never come to pass.

I was interested in the simple story of the Sell-Floto Circus and an experience that happened when the circus came to Cincinnati some years ago.

The tents were going up in a great hurry. Everyone was working hard. The manager was all but tearing his hair with nervous anxiety and haste.

A country fellow came up to the manager and asked him for a

job—"Just any kind of a job, enough to make some money to eat."

The manager, to get rid of him, said, "Well, clean out that tiger cage." He pointed to a cage of Royal Bengal tigers, four of them, and hurried away into another tent.

He had been gone about a quarter of an hour when a string of terrified employees came rushing to him, crying out, "That saphead has got all those tigers out of the cage. Come in here quick!"

The manager, with heart in throat, ran into the menagerie tent. He stood aghast at what he saw. The country boy had opened the cage, gone in, tied ropes around the necks of those beasts, led and dragged them outside and tied them to the wheels of their cage. He then had swept out the floor and put in fresh straw. Now, having untied one of the tigers, he was trying to shove him back into the cage, slapping him and growling, "Get in there, you big cat!"

Nobody dared go near, but the whole circus company stood off breathlessly and watched until all four of the angry beasts were securely back in the cage and the door shut upon them. Then the observers collapsed, and the manager gasped and made this statement, "I meant for him to take that rake and work through the bars."

That poor country boy didn't know enough to be afraid of the Bengal tigers.

We would do better if we would lose a lot of our fears and simply launch out into the deep and have faith in God.

Life is brief and uncertain, and we must not worry but trust God.

Another thought that came while my hand rested upon the cold metal of the casket:

II. HEAVEN MUST BE REAL

As I stood that day upon the sloping hillside of the cemetery, I looked upon the faces of loved ones and friends. Upon every face was a look of longing and loneliness. Each one seemed to be drinking in words of Heaven. How eagerly they accepted the thought that one day there will be a reunion with their departed loved one.

But suppose God would allow us to have such longings for Heaven, then give us no Heaven. That God would not be the God of love but the very apex of cruelty.

We must face it: if there is no Heaven, then God is cruel. He put the longing within our hearts. Then for there to be no Heaven, He would be mocking us to allow these longings to go unfulfilled.

If there is no Heaven, then Jesus lied to us; for in John 14 He said, "In my Father's house are many mansions." He gave His promise of Heaven to His disciples and to us.

If there is no Heaven, then the Bible is a fable. We had as well throw it away and forget that we ever had such a book. It would amount to nothing!

But I say to you, Heaven must be real. If there is no Heaven, if Heaven is not real, then we are of all men most miserable. And we have been mocked by our Almighty God. Heaven is real! Jesus gave proof of it by His resurrection from the grave.

But another thought came to me:

III. THESE GRAVES WILL OPEN—ALL OF THEM!

The Bible teaches the resurrection of all the dead. It does not teach that all the dead will be raised at one time.

Here is the teaching of Scripture regarding the resurrections.

First, there will be the resurrection of the saved. When Christ comes, the dead in Christ shall be raised first, and the living shall be changed, and together we shall be caught up into the air to meet the Lord. The graves of the saved will be opened.

Second, the resurrection of the unsaved will take place after the thousand-year reign of Christ on earth. The unsaved must come and stand before the Great White Throne Judgment, there to be judged and sentenced into the lake of fire forever and ever!

Go stand in the midst of the cemetery and remember these words: Every grave will open and the dead will be raised, some to life everlasting and some to eternal damnation.

This is what Daniel gives us in chapter 12:2: "And many of them that sleep in the dust of the earth shall awake, some to everlasting life, and some to shame and everlasting contempt."

This is what our Saviour was talking about when He said,

"Marvel not at this: for the hour is coming, in the which all that

are in the graves shall hear his voice, And shall come forth; they that have done good, unto the resurrection of life; and they that have done evil, unto the resurrection of damnation."—John 5:28,29.

IV. DEATH IS REAL AND DEATH IS NEAR

Go stand by the sickbed and watch a loved one slip out into eternity. Then you see that death is real.

Go to the cemetery and ponder the matter of death. Let your smile be wiped away and let your heart be filled with an earnest consideration of this matter.

Death is real! The Word of God says, "It is appointed unto men once to die, but after this the judgment."

Death is real! The Word says, "The soul that sinneth, it shall die."

Back in the book of Genesis we find the record of death as it begins. Three sad words are written after many names: ". . . and he died." The only thing that will keep you from the grave is the second coming of Jesus Christ.

Death is so real, so near. With my hand on the cold metal of the casket, I think of the nearness of death. As I look upon the bent and trembling bodies, I think, *Death is not far from any one of us.* If we live out our threescore years and ten, death is still near.

But in this present world, we are faced with death on every hand. Sudden death is common, not the exception.

Are you prepared to meet God? Do you know Christ as your Saviour? Do you have accounts of your life straightened out so that you can come into His presence?

If not, this is the moment that God has given you to make ready. I plead that you will do so today. If you have never accepted Jesus Christ as Saviour, then trust Him now.

Christian, if your life has not been counting for Him, this is the time to surrender to His will.

 **Last of All the Woman Died—
Whose Wife Shall She Be?**

"The same day came to him the Sadducees, which say that there is no resurrection, and asked him,

"Saying, Master, Moses said, If a man die, having no children, his brother shall marry his wife, and raise up seed unto his brother.

"Now there were with us seven brethren: and the first when he had married a wife, deceased, and, having no issue, left his wife unto his brother:

"Likewise the second also, and the third, unto the seventh.

"And last of all the woman died also.

"Therefore in the resurrection whose wife shall she be of the seven? for they all had her.

"Jesus answered and said unto them, Ye do err, not knowing the scriptures, nor the power of God.

"For in the resurrection they neither marry, nor are given in marriage, but are as the angels of God in heaven.

"But as touching the resurrection of the dead, have ye not read that which was spoken unto you by God, saying,

"I am the God of Abraham, and the God of Isaac, and the God of Jacob? God is not the God of the dead, but of the living.

"And when the multitude heard this, they were astonished at his doctrine."—Matt. 22:23-33.

The Lord Jesus was often faced by enemies. When He performed miracles, they found fault with Him. When He taught, they criticized His teachings. When He behaved in His natural, godly way, they accused Him of usurping authority which was not His.

The Pharisees, strict keepers of the law, disliked our Lord and were often engaged in argument with Him. The Saviour was always kind and patient; they were hotheaded and sarcastic.

The Sadducees were also in hearty disagreement with Christ. These were a small group, much smaller than the Pharisees. They began around 284 B.C. It is said that the teaching of Sadoc was the origination of their sect. It is also stated that Sadducees were usually people of some rank; therefore, it was only natural that the general public would give them some position.

What did they believe? In general, this: There is no future state, no life after this; that when the body dies, the soul is annihilated and dies with it; that there is no state of rewards or punishments in the other world; no judgment to come in Heaven or in Hell.

The Sadducees would not own the divine inspiration of the prophets nor any revelation from Heaven. The Pharisees and the Sadducees were contrary to each other, yet we notice that they often joined hands in their opposition to the Lord.

In this lesson we find our Saviour had a verbal tilt with the Sadducees. They came to Him and said:

"Master, Moses said, If a man die, having no children, his brother shall marry his wife, and raise up seed unto his brother.

"Now there were with us seven brethren: and the first, when he had married a wife, deceased, and, having no issue, left his wife unto his brother:

"Likewise the second also, and the third, unto the seventh.

"And last of all the woman died also."

The Sadducees, who did not believe in the resurrection, thought they were presenting a problem to Christ which would be quite acute: "Therefore in the resurrection whose wife shall she be of the seven?"

Let us see the answer of Jesus. First, He had to say to the Sadducees that they erred, not knowing the Scriptures nor the power of God. A man is exceedingly foolish if he endeavors to set himself up as an authority on any matter of life, if he does not know the Word of God.

Jesus gave a plain answer: "For in the resurrection they neither marry, nor are given in marriage, but are as the angels of God in heaven."

The Sadducees got their answer, but it is doubtful if they received it. Our Saviour was very positive and plain in stating that there is coming a resurrection, but in the resurrection there is no marriage, and all people who take part in the resurrection of the just will be as the angels of God in Heaven.

Now, the Sadducees could know nothing of this because they denied the power of God and the resurrection. The Bible tells us that the soul is immortal and that there is another life after this.

Ignorance of the Scriptures is the cause of the rise of much mischief. When people don't know the Word of God, whoever they may be, they will find themselves in many erroneous beliefs.

The answer of Jesus was very plain. It simply states that in the resurrection there is no marriage. In this He is stating that in Heaven there are no carnal desires, no deaths, no births, no change in the population. We become as the angels of God.

When will this change come to us? At the rapture, when the dead in Christ shall be raised and the living shall be changed. The bodies of the saints shall be raised incorruptible and glorious, and we shall be made in the likeness of our Saviour.

Now, let us come back to the story. There are three very simple things that I want you to see.

I. THE BITTER CUP OF DEATH

The story given by the Sadducees offers a picture of sadness. Death came to the seven brothers, one after the other, and last of all, to the wife.

Death will come to all of us if Christ delays His coming. The Bible tells us, "It is appointed unto men once to die, and after this the judgment."

Because death is uncertain as to time, then "prepare to meet thy God." Be ready. Don't be foolishly napping. Put your faith and trust in Jesus Christ. Rest wholly and completely in Him, and know that He will keep that which has been committed unto Him.

Again, as we think of death, we must remind ourselves that death must not cast a shadow over our lives. Some people think so much of death—it absorbs so much of their thought life—that a shadow is cast over them. This should not be. We who are the children of God should live in perfect peace and freedom of heart, unafraid, as we face the future.

Again, don't let the thought of death hinder you from doing a good work for Jesus. How foolish the person who sits down and does nothing because he thinks of death taking him away! Instead, let the fact of death give you incentive for work. Let the brevity of life drive you into greater endeavors for our Saviour.

II. THE BETTER WAY OF LIFE

Jesus said, "I am the...life." It was Paul who said, "Christ liveth in me" (Gal. 2:20).

The better way of life is in Him. He is life, He is resurrection, He is our coming King. The happy, blessed way to live is to center all of your affections, all of your thinking, in your Saviour.

It is not hard to pick out the Christ-centered person. There is a light and a life about him that radiates through all of his personality and in all of his speech. The Christ-centered life really tells in this day and time.

Dr. William Biederwolf gave a sermon years ago entitled "The Wonderful Christ." In it he stated that Jesus was wonderful in His teaching, wonderful in His works, wonderful in His influence, and wonderful in His personal claims.

"And his name shall be called Wonderful, Counsellor, the mighty God, the everlasting Father, the Prince of Peace."—Isa. 9:6.

The better way of life is to take Christ as Saviour and walk after Him. Any other pursuit brings heartache, sorrow and tears, while this brings joy, peace and comfort.

III. THE BEST IS YET TO COME

In Christ we are eternal. Our God is not the God of death, but the God of the living. We who put our faith in Jesus Christ are the sons of God, and we are eternal.

The present may be filled with heartaches and disappointments, but the future is full of joy, peace and blessedness with our Saviour.

It is in the future that we shall be free from these carnal bodies. We shall be made in His likeness. Listen to the Apostle Paul in I Corinthians 15:42-44:

"So also is the resurrection of the dead. It is sown in corruption; it is raised in incorruption:

"It is sown in dishonour; it is raised in glory: it is sown in weakness; it is raised in power:

"It is sown a natural body; it is raised a spiritual body. There is a natural body, and there is a spiritual body."

True is this Word as we think of bodies sown in corruption, decaying, but raised in incorruption, eternal. Bodies sown in dishonor, but raised in glory.

Again he says, "It is sown in weakness: it is raised in power." Now we work but a few hours, and the body tires and calls for rest; but one day it is going to be raised in power. "It is sown a natural body; it is raised a spiritual body." The natural body is subject to all of the animal appetites and passions, but the spiritual body is purified and refined.

Yes, the best is yet to come! Be not weary, be not fearful—something better is on the way!

Christ may come at any moment. When He comes, the dead in Christ shall be raised and the living shall be caught up to meet Him. If our Saviour delays His coming, we shall face death; but there is coming a resurrection day just the same. We will be present when our Lord comes again.

Many questions come to us, and we will seek for some answers. The story of the Sadducees had some puzzling questions, but Jesus answered them easily and quickly, without argument. He brought them up to the time of the resurrection and said that in the resurrection they neither marry nor are given in marriage, but are as the angels in Heaven. That is all we need.

Rest in the positive declarations of our Saviour. Do not endeavor to read into His remarks, but simply take them as given. Let His teachings give you peace and joy.

Many of you will remember the story of Ole Bull and John Erricson. Ole and John were boys together in Sweden. John was an apprentice in a mechanic shop, while Ole was learning to play the violin. They tell us that John used to say, "Ole, you had better throw that thing away. You never will amount to anything."

The two men came to this country. John Erricson grew up to be a great mechanic, and Ole Bull became a master musician, swaying the world with the power of his music.

One day Ole came to New York where John had his shop and said, "John, I want you to come down tonight to the concert hall and hear me play. Here are some tickets."

"Well, Ole," said John, "I would be glad to come, but you know I don't care for music. I have no ear for it. I couldn't appreciate it." And he didn't go.

It was a three nights' engagement. The second day John promised to go, but he didn't show.

The third day Ole said, "Now, John, you must come tonight. Come for the sake of old times together. If you don't come, I'll come out to your shop and play for you there."

John said, "No, you mustn't do that. We haven't time to listen to music; and I'll try to be there tonight." But again he failed to show up.

The next day while Ole was passing John's shop, he broke a string accidentally "on purpose." He went in and told John he wanted to fix it. While he was fixing the string, he talked to John about music, about the fibers of wood in his violin, and about harmony. Finally he said, "Let me show you, John."

As he drew the bow over the string, he made such marvelous music that John was held entranced. It floated out through the shop. The workmen lay down their tools and, drawn by an irresistible spell, crowded about as if in a dream.

You could hear the thunder of the clouds, the falling waters of the cataract in the music of the strings. He made it sob like a brokenhearted man, laugh like a dimpled-cheeked child, and sing like a nightingale in the forest. He played "America," then "Home, Sweet Home."

Suddenly he stopped. There stood John Erricson, the hard, calloused mechanic, with tears in his eyes. "Play on, Ole. Play on. I never knew what was lacking in my life before. It's music, Ole, it's music!"

There is but One who can put the joybells of Heaven to ringing within your soul. He is the One who can give you peace and joy in this life, and peace and joy throughout eternity. He is the One who can take away the fear of death. He is the One who can give you abundant life.

Will you receive Christ now as your personal Saviour?

24 The Wise Use of God's Gifts

"And I give unto them eternal life...."—John 10:28.

I have seen many a person throw away his life—a life of opportunity, a life bright with prospects of true greatness. I have seen the talented lose all because of sin. I have seen the strong go down in laziness and defeat.

There was a talented young evangelist, handsome, eloquent and educated. He possessed a winsome personality. In less than ten years his name was known in church circles throughout the nation. Then he threw it all away in sin. Death came at thirty-nine years of age.

There was a strikingly blessed minister with a unique memory. He had the ability to play many instruments and to sing beautifully. And he was a good speaker. His phenomenal memory was a great asset, but he dissipated the gifts of God. He lived for self and for ease. He refused to be stedfast. He was a quitter. He misused God's gifts. Death came while he was still young.

There was a remarkable singer with a beautiful baritone voice. He had a good range, above average volume. His musical senses were apparent. He sang with ease. He memorized without difficulty. But his failure to live for Christ was so evident that everyone knew about his weakness. So this was a talent misused.

We are touching tonight on a very important phase of life: "The wise use of God's gifts."

You will get no help from the world, the flesh or the Devil. Satan wants you to waste your life. The world will help you to throw away your talents. The flesh will accept the way of sin and weakness.

Let us consider the following:

I. THE MISUSE OF GOD'S GIFTS

God gives, but man in his weakness misuses His gifts. I can suggest just a few names, and this point of my message will be as clear as crystal.

Samson, the thirteenth judge of Israel, misused the gifts of God. The Bible tells us that "the spirit of the Lord was upon him." He had a God-given strength. He had a faith in the living God.

Samson allowed sin to come into his life. He behaved wickedly, and then came the end. His eyes were put out by the Philistines, and he was made to grind in the prison house.

The only redeeming picture is in the closing of this man's life when the strength of God came upon him again and he conquered the Philistines in one supreme moment.

David misused the gifts of God. This man was so blessed of the Lord. It seemed that everything he did had a touch of Heaven upon it.

Then came the day when David slipped away from the side of God and fell into sin. He lost much of the glory which had been attached to his name.

Solomon misused the gifts of God. He was signally blessed of God with wisdom. Portions of the greatest book in the world came from the hand of Solomon, inspired of God. Yet Solomon misused the gifts God had given him. The story of part of his declension is given to us in I Kings 11:3, 4:

"And he had seven hundred wives, princesses, and three hundred concubines: and his wives turned away his heart. For it came to pass, when Solomon was old, that his wives turned away his heart after other gods: and his heart was not perfect with the Lord his God, as was the heart of David his father."

Hezekiah misused the gifts of God. He was a great king. When death was near, he prayed; and God gave him an additional fifteen years.

But during this time, the king exposed his treasures to the

men of Babylon, misusing the time given him.

Ananias and Sapphira misused the gifts of God. I believe that these two had been saved. It is evident that they had wealth. They were in fellowship with the people in the early church. They had the opportunity for doing much good, but they misused God's gifts when they lied to the Holy Spirit. As a consequence, both died.

So many people misuse the gifts of God. They put on a front and appear to have much when they have nothing.

Some years ago a tornado tore through Nashville, Tennessee. When I heard the roaring force of the wind and the awful devastation brought about by it, I stopped my car and waited until the storm had gone by. Then I walked into the area touched by the fury of the storm. I tried to help people in their distress.

I think one of the strangest things that I saw, in the midst of all the destruction of houses, was a front door standing—unbroken. The front of the house was left, but inside there was nothing.

Some people are like that door. Their words, their looks, their manners are delightful; but their hearts are empty. They have not allowed the Lord to reign as King of kings and Lord of lords.

Oh, the curse of the misused life!

A minister was asked by a brokenhearted mother to visit her son in a penitentiary. She handed the minister her photograph with a letter and said, "Will you show him my picture? He never answers my letters. Maybe this will touch his heart."

The man called the prison, and the young man was brought in under guard. Upon being presented with a photograph, he said without emotion, "Yes, that's my mother. Her hair is more gray but that's her." Then handing the photograph back, along with the letter (which he refused to read), he said in a voice full of bitterness: "When you see her again, return these. I don't want them. It was in my mother's home I played the first game of cards, and it was she who gave me my first drink. Those two things, drinking and gambling, have put me here for fifteen years. And now she sends me a picture with belated love. Take them back and tell her that I hate both her and the religion she professes!"

Be careful, my friend, how you use your life, your influence.

II. THE WISE USE OF GOD'S GIFTS

How good the Lord has been to every one of us! How abundant are His blessings to us! May God open our eyes to see the many things that He has done in our behalf.

What gifts has He given us?

First, the gift of salvation. Jesus said, "And I give unto them eternal life; and they shall never perish, neither shall any man pluck them out of my hand" (John 10:28).

Paul said, "For the wages of sin is death; but the gift of God is eternal life through Jesus Christ our Lord" (Rom. 6:23).

In Ephesians 2:8, 9 we read, "For by grace are ye saved through faith; and that not of yourselves: it is the gift of God: Not of works, lest any man should boast."

How we should praise God for the gift of everlasting life! In this strange day, it is so difficult to find people who give any sensible expression of their gratitude for the gift of salvation.

A few days ago I made a call to one of our local hospitals, visiting a lady of advanced years. I had been told that she was a Christian. When I stood by the bedside and asked her again, "Friend, have you been saved? Are you a child of God?" she flippantly answered, "Oh, yes, of course."

An old man used to carry a book with him, which he very often took from his pocket to show to others. He called it his "Biography." It had only three leaves. Not a word was written on any of them, yet he said it contained the whole story of his life.

The first leaf was black—that, he said, was his sin, his condition by nature. The second was red—that, he told them, represented the blood of Christ. The third was white—that final page, he said, stood for himself—washed in that blood and made whiter than snow.

Have you been cleansed by the precious blood of the Lord Jesus Christ?

Second, the gift of the Holy Spirit. When you got saved, He entered in. Now recognize the Holy Spirit. Let Him fill you, possess you, guide you. Don't grieve the Holy Spirit by wrongdoing (Eph. 4:30-32). Don't quench the Holy Spirit by refusing to follow His guidance. Let the Spirit of God fill you, possess you and direct all your activities.

Third, the gift of peace. Jesus said, "My peace I give unto you." Use very wisely this gift, for it is this that will keep you steady in the time of storm. It is this that will give you confidence when all else fails.

We have been hearing about the hijacking of a number of airplanes. Scores have been placed into positions of danger. Death has been close to many. I wonder how many of that crowd understand the peace of God!

Some years ago an artist painted a picture entitled "The Peace of God." On the stone floor of an old dungeon, two women were seen to be fast asleep, their hands joined together. One was white and very beautiful; the other was black and clad in the garments of a slave. They were evidently mistress and servant.

Something else: Because they were Christians and would not renounce their faith in Christ, they had been cast into this dungeon.

In the very room where they were confined might be seen the lion's cage. In it were three full-grown beasts who had been made furious by days of fasting. Tomorrow they would break their fast on the bodies of these helpless victims.

The artist gave us a vision of their eyes glaring in the darkness. The women who had been cast in prison knew well enough that tomorrow they must die, just as many of their friends had perished before them in those dark and terrible days of persecution. But in spite of that, they had lain down on the stone floor and were sleeping as calmly as a child might sleep locked in the embrace of her mother's arms.

This is the gift of peace that we are talking about. When we are in Christ, we possess a peace that "passeth all understanding." Those with this peace are making their ways from earth to Heaven with the joy of the Lord in their souls.

Peace, sweet peace, is the gift of God!

D. L. Moody used to tell about a scene on a battlefield during the War Between the States. Administering to the wounded and dying, he came to a soldier and passed him by because he was motionless. Then soon, when he saw a hand move slightly, he turned back to him, lifted his head, wet his lips and asked the soldier if there was anything he could do for him.

In faint tones he answered, "Get the Book out of my pocket and read to me."

Moody took a Testament out of the soldier's pocket, opened it and asked: "What shall I read?"

"Read the fourteenth chapter of John."

Moody began. The soldier closed his eyes. Moody read on and on. When he came to the words, "Peace I leave with you, my peace I give unto you: not as the world giveth, give I unto you. Let not your heart be troubled, neither let it be afraid," the soldier opened his eyes and said, "That will do, Chaplain. I have that peace."

May the peace of God steady your heart in these troubled days.

Fourth, the gift of the Bible. This Word has come to us from the hand of God. This divine Book is His gift to us. How are you using it? Do you love the Word of God?

> Holy Bible, Book divine,
> Precious treasure, thou art mine;
> Mine to tell me whence I came,
> Mine to teach me what I am.
>
> Mine to tell of joys to come
> And the rebel sinner's doom.
> Oh, thou holy Book divine,
> Precious treasure, thou art mine.

Fifth, the gift of life and opportunity. We have it now! This moment is a gift from Him.

Think of the gift of time—"redeeming the time, because the days are evil."

Time is not wasted when we pray.

Time is not wasted when we worship.

Time is not wasted when we study the Word of God.

Time is not wasted when we meditate upon the goodness of God.

But time is wasted when we engage in sin, when we languish in laziness, when we lie in the hogpens of this world.

God has given us time—precious time. May we use it for holy

purposes, for prayer, Bible study, worship, meditation, soul winning.

Now, how shall we use these gifts which come from our Lord? How blessed to remember the wealth which is ours.

First, give thanks to God for His gifts. "Thanks be unto God for his unspeakable gift," said Paul, referring to the gift of salvation. But we should be grateful for every gift our Lord gives us.

Second, share with others. The entire gospel theme means sharing. Since we have been blessed, then we must let others know of God's blessings upon us.

Again, show forth Christ. So live that others can see Christ in us.

I read about a little girl who was busy one day with a pencil and paper. "What are you doing?" asked her mother.

"Making a picture of God."

"But," said the shocked mother, "you can't do that. You have never seen God. Nobody has ever seen God. Nobody knows what God is like."

The little girl was in no wise discouraged. Licking her pencil and bending over her paper, she answered, "They will know when I am finished with this."

The child was not speaking as foolishly as the mother thought. Each day by deeds and words we are painting a picture of Christ for others to hold. Paul wrote to the Corinthians, "Ye are our epistles...known and read of all men."

Therefore, I exhort you to use wisely the gifts of God. Use what you have in holy pursuits.

III. THE REWARD FOR THE FAITHFUL

First, there is a reward now. When we use God's gifts properly, there are blessings at this moment: abundant rewards now, the presence of God. He commends my faithfulness and reproves me when I follow afar off. Weary at times? Yes. Discouraged at times? Yes. But my Lord is with me, and I enjoy the blessings of His presence.

A pastor in a New England town became discouraged and weary. With a sense of failure, he climbed to the steeple room in his church to think. Though he was a man of God, yet he felt he had failed. Perhaps if he had been an unconverted person, he might have attempted suicide. But this man, Washington Gladden, stepped up and poured out his heart to the Lord in prayer. Then he wrote this hymn: "Oh, Master, Let Me Walk With Thee."

> Oh, Master, let me walk with Thee
> In lowly paths of service free.
> Tell me Thy secret, help me to bear
> The strain of toil, the fret of care.
>
> Help me the slow of heart to move
> By some clear, winning word of love.
> Teach me the wayward feet to stay
> And guide them in the homeward way.
>
> Teach me Thy patience! Still with Thee
> In closer, dearer company,
> In work that keeps faith sweet and strong,
> In trust that triumphs over wrong.
>
> In hope that sends a shining ray
> Far down the future's broadening way,
> In peace that only Thou canst give,
> With Thee, oh, Master, let me live.

But not only is there a reward now for faithfulness, there is a future reward. There is coming a judgment seat, when we shall stand before our Lord. The apostle said, "For we must all appear before the judgment seat of Christ." We shall stand there to give an account of ourselves unto Him. In that day, every man's work shall be made manifest. If our works abide, we receive a reward. If they be burned, we suffer loss, yet we shall be saved "so as by fire."

I don't think we should fear the judgment seat, but I do think we should be ready. Let us examine our hearts daily to make sure we are ready to stand before Him. Perhaps some people need to ask the question of the song:

> Must I go, and empty-handed,
>   Thus my dear Redeemer meet?
> Not one day of service give Him,
>   Lay no trophy at His feet?
>
> Must I go, and empty-handed?
>   Must I meet my Saviour so?
> Not one soul with which to greet Him—
>   Must I empty-handed go?

The story is told of how Queen Victoria was listening to the palace chaplain preach a sermon on the significance of the second coming of Christ. The people near the royal box noticed that the queen was shaking, that her lips quivered, and that her eyes were filled with tears.

When the service was ended, she asked to see the chaplain alone. Observing her great emotion, he asked why she was so moved. Her reply: "Oh, sir, because of what you said about the coming of the world's rightful King, I could wish still to be here when He returns, that I might lay my crown at His blessed feet!"

He is coming! Are you ready? Are you using the gifts of God?

We have spoken of the gift of salvation, the gift of the Holy Spirit, the gift of peace, the gift of the Book, and the gift of time. Are you faithful in the use of these gifts?

Perhaps tonight there is someone who has never accepted Jesus Christ as his own personal Saviour. You have no witness of the Christ in your heart. God has been good to you in that He has allowed you to live to this moment. You are in this service tonight for a purpose. Surely God desires that you receive His Son and be saved.

Perhaps there are many of you Christians who testify to your salvation, but yet you have not used in a wise way the gifts of God. Come in complete surrender to Him in this moment.

25 My Deepest Sympathy

"Then in the audience of all the people he said unto his disciples,

"Beware of the scribes, which desire to walk in long robes, and love greetings in the markets, and the highest seats in the synagogues, and the chief rooms at feasts;

"Which devour widows' houses, and for a shew make long prayers: The same shall receive greater damnation."—Luke 20:45-47.

". . . be thou faithful unto death, and I will give thee a crown of life."—Rev. 2:10.

Most of us agree that one should have sympathy for the bereaved. The Saviour's heart was touched by the sorrow of others.

When Jesus saw the widow of Nain walking with the body of her departed son, He was sorrowful and raised the boy to life and restored him to his mother.

The Saviour was touched by the death of Lazarus and the sorrow expressed by the sisters. "Jesus wept." Even though He knew He would raise Lazarus from the dead, He sympathized nonetheless.

Expressing sympathy in the death of others should not be hard but should be a definite part of our relationship toward others.

The sick and the afflicted should have our sympathy. The heart of Jesus was touched by the needs of people. No needy person was ever brought before Him without the touch of His healing hand. When the palsied man came before the Lord, Jesus said to him, "Son, thy sins be forgiven thee." Then when He saw the people reasoning in their hearts and saying, "Why doth this man thus speak blasphemies?

Who can forgive sins but God only?" Jesus told the sick man to arise and take up his bed and walk. Our Master always had sympathy for the sick and troubled.

Again, our sympathy should be with those going through deep waters. The trouble may be in the home, between husband and wife, or between parents and children, or even financial. As it was with Jesus, so should it be with us.

Again, the honest doubter should have our sympathy. Doubting Thomas was never criticized by our Lord. Rather, Christ sought to help him and endeavored to establish his faith. So should it be with us.

But now I speak of three special classes of people who should touch the hearts of all Christians.

I. SYMPATHY FOR THE SARCASTIC

Jesus spoke sharply to the Pharisees in Matthew 23, but He spoke in love. His heart was touched as He saw the masses of these religious leaders refuse Him.

The Pharisees were often sarcastic. They criticized the Saviour and His ministry. They sought to trap Him in various statements. They found fault with Him when He healed people. They criticized His use of the Sabbath day. They tried in every conceivable fashion to catch our Saviour in some mistake, but they failed.

Did Jesus love the Pharisees? Yes. After giving severe condemnation of their sins as found in Matthew 23, we find the Saviour weeping over Jerusalem, the city which had refused Him and the salvation He offered.

So should it be with us. Our hearts should be moved by the sarcastic, those people lost and undone, without God, without hope in the world. The sarcastic one is calling out of an empty heart; or conviction is upon him, and his sarcasm comes because of his convicted heart.

Sarcasm expresses itself usually in biting and cold words. Let us be careful that we are touched with a heavenly sympathy for those bound by the sin of sarcasm.

"Let me look at your tongue" is quite often the first word of a physician to one who is sick. The tongue, the doctor knows, is a sure test of a condition of one's bodily health. In like manner, the tongue is a good test of the condition of one's heart and soul. If the tongue is sharp and biting, sarcastic and cruel, there is a need—perhaps a need of salvation.

For many years I fought a battle with myself regarding sarcastic people. I was inclined to answer sarcasm with sarcasm. Now I am conscious of what is right.

May our hearts be touched with sympathy for the sarcastic.

II. SYMPATHY FOR THE HARDHEARTED

My heart goes out to the hardhearted.

The Herodians in the time of Christ seemed pictured by that expression. They did not assume the sarcastic attitudes of the Pharisees, but their antireligious expression seemed to be one of hardness.

What is it that makes people hardhearted?

First, it is sin. Sin always hardens the heart. When one constantly engages in evil, he will turn away from Christ and from right thinking on spiritual truths.

Second, hardheartedness comes because of rejection of Christ. The first rejection may be somewhat difficult, but after awhile it is easy for one to say no to salvation. I have met in this church and in revival meetings some who could smile and say no to accepting Christ just as easily as they might refuse some small gift. Hearts become hard when people continue to reject the Lord Jesus Christ.

Again, hardheartedness comes because of poor examples of Christianity. Some turn away from Christ and salvation because they see no real demonstration of it in those near them. A lad turns away from Christ when he sees in his father such a poor example of what it means to be a Christian. A husband turns away from God and Christ because his wife, a professing Christian, demonstrates so poorly what it means to be born again.

Perhaps the most hardhearted man I ever met lived near the first church that I pastored. His wife and daughter belonged to the church, and they attended when it pleased them. They were folks of some culture and aristocracy.

One day I went to talk with the man about his soul. The wife and daughter sat in one part of the room. As I dealt with him, he said, "I might be inclined to hear what you have to say if I could see just one demonstration of a Christian life." When he said this, his wife and daughter, convicted, left the room.

This man was hardhearted. Why? Because he had seen such poor examples of what it means to be a Christian.

Is there any hope? Yes, for some of the hardhearted there will come a day when the heart is made soft. It may take illness, sudden calamity, the death of loved ones, financial reverses; but there will come a time when the ears will listen to the message of salvation.

Listen to Job 23:16: "For God maketh my heart soft, and the Almighty troubleth me." God knows how to soften the heart. He can make it receive His Word. The Lord knows exactly how and what to do.

A soldier was dying on the field of battle. The chaplain was bending over him. The soldier gasped, "Give me a light, Chaplain."

The chaplain reached into the soldier's pocket, took out a cigarette, put it between his lips, and was about to strike the match when the soldier said, "The other kind of light, Chaplain."

The chaplain reached into his pocket, took out his New Testament, and began to read, "Let not your heart be troubled: ye believe in God, believe also in me. In my Father's house are many mansions: if it were not so, I would have told you. I go to prepare a place for you."

He read on. After awhile the soldier sighed and said, "That's it, Chaplain!" In a few moments he was dead.

The need of man is Christ. Let your hard heart be broken up by the message of our Christ.

III. SYMPATHY FOR THE UNFAITHFUL

We are thinking now of the man who has been saved by the precious blood of Jesus Christ—the man whose name is written down in the Lamb's book of life, and yet he is unfaithful.

Such a one has often stirred the wrong emotion within my heart. I have tried to think that it was righteous indignation, but I doubt that. I have asked God to help me. Now my heart goes out to unfaithful ones.

A man may be unfaithful in the use of his time or money or talents. Let us be careful to have toward this one a feeling of love, then endeavor to help him.

The unfaithful miss the joy of service. Is there anything greater in this world than serving Jesus?

They miss the joy of doing their best for Christ. We can always walk off the field of battle with a feeling of joy and satisfaction. We may have lost the game, but we still can feel that it was worthwhile—that is, when we have done our best.

The unfaithful miss the joy of fellowship. Fellowship comes when we walk and talk with our Saviour. Fellowship cannot be enjoyed when we are walking afar off. It comes as we abide in Him and as we obey His every command.

The unfaithful miss the best now and when Christ comes. When we stand before the judgment seat, it is then that the unfaithful must give an account of himself to God. In that day, lies, deception, hypocrisy will not avail—only the truth then. The excuses of man will disappear. Yes, the unfaithful miss the best now and the best when Jesus comes.

What will be the best in that day? To hear Him say, "Well done, thou good and faithful servant."

In closing, what does the unfaithful need?

First, a consciousness that men may stumble into Hell because of his example. Oh, that God would grant some way to drive this into your heart! Mothers and fathers, will you not see that? Your bad example may send your children to an everlasting Hell. Young man, will you not see that? Your bad example may cause others to be lost. Let the cry of Paul ring in your ears: "Destroy not him with thy meat, for whom Christ died."

Live so others can see Christ in you. Unfaithful one, open your eyes and see that men may stumble into Hell because of your example.

Second, the consciousness that Christ is looking down on the unfaithful. If this solemn thought ever gets hold of your heart, you will never be the same. That our Christ is watching your every act, that He knows your thoughts, that He understands your strengths and failures—this can both encourage and awaken us.

Be encouraged to know that Christ is watching what you are doing. Be awakened from drowsiness and from indifference by the consciousness that He sees and knows what you are.

Third, the consciousness that life is short and time is fleeting. What we do must be done now. We have no promise of any certain length of days. The need of activity is now. The need for diligence is today. The time for service is at this moment.

May God grant to each one of us the Spirit of Christ and the attitudes of our Saviour toward others. Let your prayer be, "O God, make me a faithful Christian!"

If you have never accepted Christ, then turn to Him at this time.

 **The Great Question and the Great Answer**

"How shall this be. . . ?"—Luke 1:34.

"The Holy Ghost shall come upon thee. . . ."—Luke 1:35.

"For with God nothing shall be impossible."—Luke 1:37.

"But ye are not in the flesh, but in the Spirit, if so be that the Spirit of God dwell in you. Now if any man have not the Spirit of Christ, he is none of his."—Rom. 8:9.

It will profit us to notice the Holy Spirit as He is mentioned in Luke 1.

Regarding John the Baptist, the angel of the Lord said before he was born:

"For he shall be great in the sight of the Lord, and shall drink neither wine nor strong drink; and he shall be filled with the Holy Ghost, even from his mother's womb."—Luke 1:15.

The angel said unto Mary: "The Holy Ghost shall come upon thee, and the power of the Highest shall overshadow thee: therefore also that holy thing which shall be born of thee shall be called the Son of God" (Luke 1:35).

In verse 41 are these words: "And it came to pass, that, when Elisabeth heard the salutation of Mary, the babe leaped in her womb; and Elisabeth was filled with the Holy Ghost."

In verse 67 we find these words regarding Zacharias: "And his father Zacharias was filled with the Holy Ghost, and prophesied. . . ."

Returning now for just a moment to the story of Mary, we do not wonder that she asked the question, "How shall this be?" She had been told by the angel that she would bear a child and His name would be called Jesus and that He would reign upon the throne of David and over the house of Jacob forever. And she cried out, "How shall this be, seeing I know not a man?"

I believe that this was a question of awestruck inquiry, not one of unbelief.

The angel gave the answer unto Mary: "The Holy Ghost shall come upon thee, and the power of the Highest shall overshadow thee...."

I give emphasis in this message to the work of the Holy Spirit. There are mighty things that God would have each of us do; and sometimes, like Mary, we may be saying, "How shall this be?" However, it may be that we will be asking the question with much doubt, even as Zacharias, when the Lord came unto him. But the question should be asked in simple, believing faith.

Now, consider three things:

I. THE DESIRE FOR THE OVERCOMING LIFE

Every Christian desires to be victorious. He may not always say it, and he may not understand the way to victory; but in his heart he wants to live a victorious life.

This is exactly what Paul said he wanted. Notice these words:

"Know ye not that they which run in a race run all, but one receiveth the prize? So run, that ye may obtain.

"And every man that striveth for the mastery is temperate in all things. Now they do it to obtain a corruptible crown; but we an incorruptible.

"I therefore so run, not as uncertainly; so fight I, not as one that beateth the air:

"But I keep under my body, and bring it into subjection: lest that by any means, when I have preached to others, I myself should be a castaway."—I Cor. 9:24-27.

Paul knew that in himself he was a defeated man.

Paul knew that in the flesh he could not be victorious. In Romans 7 he said:

"For I know that in me (that is, in my flesh,) dwelleth no good thing: for to will is present with me; but how to perform that which is good I find not. For the good that I would I do not: but the evil which I would not, that I do."—Vss. 18,19.

Paul came to the only conclusion that anyone can come to: If we are to be victorious, it must be by the Holy Spirit in us.

He wrote to the people in Rome, "Likewise the Spirit also helpeth our infirmities..." (Rom. 8:26).

See sin for what it is. In the miserable weakness of our time, men are turning away from Christ, from holiness, from purity of life.

For example, in London, in one of the Anglican churches, beer and liquor are now being served. What a tragedy that a church designed to preach the Bible and point people to Heaven would become the means of sending young people to Hell!

I repeat: see sin for what it is.

The *Atlanta Constitution* for Wednesday, March 6, 1968, had a seven-column write-up on "Student Co-Habitation Reflects Insecurity at U.S. Colleges." The article tells how in United States colleges many young people are living together without marriage. The article tells about a number of couples in various colleges who have their apartments and live together with their children but never become husband and wife in the official or religious sense.

One of the deans at Columbia said, "It reflects what is happening in America today—the breakdown of Victorian and Protestant ethics, the creation of a whole new set of values, and a new emphasis on honesty and integrity in interpersonal relationships."

Face it! It is simply plain, old sin—the same they had in Sodom and Gomorrah.

It is pathetic that our educators, religious leaders and nation give approval to such sinful wickedness and take no steps to correct it.

There is one source of overcoming strength—the indwelling Holy Spirit. In yourself you are a defeated person; in Christ, you are a conqueror.

Let me suggest these three things to every person:

First, examine your own salvation. Know beyond a shadow of a doubt that you are saved. This Bible tells us that we can know we have passed from death unto life. John said, "He that hath the Son hath life; and he that hath not the Son of God hath not life" (I John 5:12).

Second, desire to be victorious. You may receive Jesus Christ as your Saviour, but you will not live an overcoming life until you desire this.

I talked to a lady a few days ago. She testified to her salvation, but she confessed that she was living a defeated life. And the tragedy was, she had no desire to be a victorious Christian.

Third, let the Holy Spirit give you power to overcome. Jesus said, "But ye shall receive power, after that the Holy Ghost is come upon you . . ." (Acts 1:8). I know quite well that the Saviour meant that by the power of the Holy Spirit we could be witnesses for Him in all parts of the world. But I understand also that we can only be witnesses when the Holy Spirit gives us power to be overcomers. You can conquer in Him. You can find in Him all you need for daily living.

There is power for every Christian in this building. The overcoming life is yours if you will let the Holy Spirit fill, pervade and dominate your life.

Charles Haddon Spurgeon was troubled one day about a problem; then the words of II Corinthians 12:9 came to him: "My grace is sufficient for thee." Spurgeon began to imagine. He felt he was transported to the bank of a flowing river. He saw a little fish drinking away; then all of a sudden the fish stopped and said, "I mustn't take too much, or there will be none left." The river replied, "Drink on, little fish: my waters are sufficient for thee."

Then Mr. Spurgeon said that he imagined that he was standing beside one of Joseph's great granaries in Egypt. A little mouse was feeding there. It stopped its meal and said, "I must not eat too much now, or there will not be enough for tomorrow." But the storehouse answered, "Feed on, little mouse: my grain is sufficient for thee."

Next, Spurgeon said he imagined himself on the top of a great mountain. He saw a man filling his lungs with the refreshing, invigorating air. But the man stopped and said, "I must be careful not to use up too much oxygen, or there will be no supply for future needs." The vast mountain amusingly replied, "Breathe on, little man: my winds are sufficient for thee."

Then Charles Haddon Spurgeon said he was brought back to the great text, "My grace is sufficient for thee."

God has enough for everyone. He has all the power we need, all the grace we need, all the strength we will ever need for any conflict.

So have a desire for the overcoming life.

II. THE DESIRE FOR A WELL-SPENT LIFE

How? By the Holy Spirit.

What a tragedy to see so many young people—yes, and older ones, too—wasting their lives in the hogpens of the world!

Plain, open sin is causing many to waste their lives. It may be a sin of stealing, cheating, immorality, robbing God or robbing another. Sin brings waste.

Selfishness causes some to waste their lives. They are going after the things they want, trying to satisfy their own desires. This is a great battle with all of us.

Many lives are wasted in useless endeavors. It is appalling how many spend themselves in doing that which means nothing at all.

Determine to use your life in the proper way. This, too, can only be done by careful consideration of what God has done and by recognition of the Holy Spirit who abides within. When you got saved, He took up His residence in your heart and is there for good to make your life count for God.

First, take time to remember that you are indwelt by the Holy Spirit. He indwells you to lead you. Romans 8:14: "For as many as are led by the Spirit of God, they are the sons of God."

Second, take time to pray. No one can achieve usefulness without prayer. This is the mainspring of life. Prayer is our privilege, and a most exacting test.

In an African village, a number of Christians used to go to a certain spot in the forest for their daily prayer. They say that it was interesting to observe how, in the course of time, the grass was worn down into a track leading from each Christian hut to the place of prayer. Sometimes when one of them would grow slack, his track would begin to show signs of disuse. One of the others would then say to the backsliding member, "Brother, there is grass on your track."

Exercise care that you do not let grass grow on your track.

Third, take time to wait for His direction. He will direct into the way you should take.

Fourth, be sure that your influence is counting for Christ. No life is well spent when that life is used by Satan to lead others astray. So live that people will see Christ in you and will want to follow Him. Avoid even that which seems harmless if it would hurt someone else.

A young man made his way to a city for a new appointment in the business world. After getting his lodging, he began walking around downtown. He saw the entrance to the motion picture house. But he remembered that his Christian parents had warned him against the sin of worldly motion pictures and told him he should not be found in such a place.

But as he stood there, he saw a man who had on a ministerial collar walk up, pay his money and go inside. The young man thought, *If it's all right for him, it's all right for me.*

That single step led him down to a life of sin.

Because of his sin, he later became quite ill. His landlady asked if he would like to have a minister come and pray with him. Yes, he would.

In a few hours there came to his room the very minister he had followed into the motion picture house—the one who had, some time back, caused him to become loose in his living.

Let your influence be positive and radiant for Christ. Get your inspiration for Christian living from the Word of God. You can't find it on television.

The Episcopal church is putting out a series for television entitled "One Reach One." One part of the series is entitled "Love in a Sexy Society." Even *Time* magazine says that the series presents "a realism that is almost painful."

A Southern Baptist minister, Clarence Jordan, has written what he calls "The Cotton Patch Version of Paul's Epistles." This has recently been published by the Y.M.C.A.

Jordan said, "The Scripture should be taken out of the stained-glass sanctuary and put out under God's skies." The trouble with it is, Jordan's translation is low, vile, vulgar and far from true to the original versions. Much of it is vulgarity.

Now I impress upon you the second point—the desire for a well-spent life. Don't waste your life in sin. Spend it in activities directed by the Holy Spirit who indwells you.

III. THE DESIRE FOR A FRUITFUL LIFE

How is this to be obtained? The Holy Spirit, the One who indwells you, will guide you into fruitful living.

One Bible teacher has taken the portion in Galatians 5:19-26 and has called this: "From the Slum to the Orchard."

On the side of the slums we find adultery, fornication, uncleanness, lasciviousness, idolatry, witchcraft, hatred, variance, emulations, wrath, strife, seditions, heresies, envyings, murders, drunkenness, revellings and such like.

But when we turn the corner, we find, "But the fruit of the Spirit is love, joy, peace, longsuffering, gentleness, goodness, faith, Meekness, temperance..." (Gal. 5:22,23).

How sad that some people live in the slums and do the works of the flesh instead of coming into God's orchard and bearing the fruit of the Spirit!

Second, we must bear the fruit of souls. Perhaps you are saying, "I have no longing to win souls." Then this must be evidence of a spiritual need. When we have the fullness of the Holy Spirit, we will want to bring people to the Lord.

Jesus said, "Wherefore by their fruits ye shall know them" (Matt. 7:20). Are you bearing the fruit of the Spirit? Bearing the fruit of souls?

Could your failure to win souls and be interested in others be the result of not being filled with the Holy Spirit?

I am trying to emphasize the great need for the filling of the

Spirit. How will I have a desire for the overcoming life, a desire to spend my life in the right way, a desire for a fruitful life? Just one way only—by being filled with the Holy Spirit.

This is a strange world in which we are living—a world of rockets flashing around through the atmosphere; a world in which airplanes can carry seven hundred or more passengers and tons and tons of cargo; a world in which men are doing strange things. The governor of Florida, though failing in his handling of the teacher situation, has given his approval to the building of a hotel on the bottom of the ocean! He thinks it would be great for people to spend a few days at the bottom of the sea where they can study sea life and the beauties of the ocean.

What we need is a return to simple Bible teaching.

In this matter of the Holy Spirit's work, I think of three great hours. The first was years ago in Louisville, Kentucky, when I heard a message on the Scripture, "Christ liveth in me," from Galatians 2:20. The contemplation of that theme did something for me. I have never forgotten it.

The second great hour of my life came in a city a few hundred miles from here. I was in the midst of a revival meeting. God had to bring me down and almost put me on the shelf so that He could teach me the lesson of the fullness of the Holy Spirit.

The third great hour was when I caught hold of the truth of "dying to self." I read the little books by a Scottish author, *When Did You Die?* and *How to Die Daily.* The simple thoughts of these books pointed me to a great and important teaching. I had to come and say with Paul, "I die daily."

I have given this message in the hope of helping some Christian. If you have never been saved, then, of course, your first need is to repent of sin and believe in Jesus Christ.

27 The Holy Spirit and You

"Howbeit when he, the Spirit of truth, is come, he will guide you into all truth: for he shall not speak of himself; but whatsoever he shall hear, that shall he speak: and he will shew you things to come."—John 16:13.

The entire message of the Holy Spirit fails unless your heart is touched and moved.

If we consider this matter academically, we have done no more than one who considers the climate of Haiti or the rainfall in Africa. If we consider this matter experimentally, seeking something for ourselves, we may arrive at some good but fail to know the true significance of the message of the Holy Spirit.

This subject must be dealt with in a scriptural and spiritual way.

What does the Bible say about the Holy Spirit? What does your heart say about Him? What do you know about the Holy Spirit?

First, we must acknowledge that there is a Holy Spirit! Jesus Himself gave witness to this and mentions the Father, the Son and the Holy Spirit. The Word of God has much to say regarding the Holy Spirit. The Holy Spirit filled and empowered our Saviour when He was led into the wilderness. And Christ did His work in the power of the Spirit.

But we must remember that the Old Testament records the action of the Holy Spirit. We find that He was active in creation:

"In the beginning God created the heaven and the earth. And the earth was without form, and void; and darkness was upon the face

of the deep. And the Spirit of God moved upon the face of the waters."—Gen. 1:1,2.

Throughout the Old Testament the Holy Spirit moved upon the hearts of men and led them at various times in works of divine grace. The Holy Spirit was always striving with men and seeking to lead them unto higher planes.

The great revivals in Old Testament days were wrought by the Spirit of God. We read in Zechariah 4:6, "Not by might, nor by power, but by my spirit, saith the Lord of hosts."

In the messages of the prophets, the Spirit worked. In the dark hours when God brought forth His great men, the Holy Spirit empowered them for denouncing sin and announcing the purpose of God.

But it was in the New Testament that the Holy Spirit came upon men to abide. The Spirit of God was in evidence in the time of John the Baptist and the Lord Jesus, then on the day of Pentecost when He came in power upon the disciples and they testified and many were turned to the Lord Jesus.

Yes, we must know the work of the Holy Spirit in olden days.

Second, we must understand His work today. He convicts men of sin (John 16:8). He converts (John 3:5). He comforts (Rom. 8:26, 27). He aids in the time of weakness.

The work of the Holy Spirit is for everyone—for men and women, for preachers, for laymen.

His work will cure shallowness, one of the sins of America. We have come to the sad day when people join churches but do not join the Lord Jesus Christ. We live in a time when the doctrine of the Holy Spirit is despised and disregarded.

The work of the Holy Spirit will cure self-seeking, a chief sin which afflicts both the ministry and laymen. Preachers will sell their souls for a high position.

Again, the work of the Holy Spirit will quench faultfinding. Real sin needs to be condemned, but imaginary ills can be left alone when we are under the domination of the Holy Spirit.

Three things we must know regarding the Holy Spirit and His work.

I. HE INDWELLS BELIEVERS

When we are saved, the Spirit of God comes in and takes up His abode in our hearts and lives.

Notice John 14:16,17:

"And I will pray the Father, and he shall give you another Comforter, that he may abide with you for ever; Even the Spirit of truth; whom the world cannot receive, because it seeth him not, neither knoweth him: but ye know him; for he dwelleth with you, and shall be in you."

And read Romans 8:9:

"But ye are not in the flesh, but in the Spirit, if so be that the Spirit of God dwell in you. Now if any man have not the Spirit of Christ, he is none of his."

If you are a believer, then the Spirit of God dwells in you. In I Corinthians 3:16 Paul was talking to baby Christians—those who had not grown in the Lord—when he said, "Ye are the temple of God, and the Spirit of God dwelleth in you." Perhaps there are some here who have not grown in grace. You are still babes in Christ. Nevertheless, the Spirit of God dwells within you.

Though you are still walking and talking as a babe, there is evidence in your souls that you are a child of God. This evidence comes by the Holy Spirit: "The Spirit itself beareth witness with our spirit, that we are the children of God" (Rom. 8:16).

II. HE WORKS THROUGH BELIEVERS

The Holy Spirit is that inner voice correcting us, guiding us, directing us in the Lord's work.

First, it is when we live for God in a clean and upright fashion that the Spirit of God can work through us. Do not expect the Holy Spirit to do His work when there is filth and dirt inside.

Second, He leads us: "For as many as are led by the Spirit of God, they are the sons of God" (Rom. 8:14). Paul gives us such a complete illustration of this. His desire was to go from Mysia to Bithynia, but the Spirit suffered him not.

How wise to wait upon the Holy Spirit for leading and direction! What mistakes we will avoid if we will simply wait for His hand to guide us!

Third, the Spirit works through us in positive witnessing.

On the notable day of Pentecost, when the disciples were filled with the Holy Spirit, they began to speak with other tongues, telling of the Lord Jesus Christ. In the company there were those who understood the tongues which they used.

They gave such a positive message of our Saviour that three thousand accepted Jesus Christ and followed Him in baptism on that day. At another time five thousand were saved. Thousands united with the church in Jerusalem.

How did it happen? All the Christians were busy witnessing for Christ.

If you are a believer, He dwells within you. Now, give way to His presence. Let His power work through you. Let the Spirit operate through you.

It was Charles Haddon Spurgeon who said:

> If we do not have the Spirit of God, it were better to shut the churches, to nail up the doors, to put a black cross upon them and say, "God have mercy upon us!"
>
> If you ministers have not the Spirit of God, you had better not preach and your people had better stay at home.
>
> I think I speak not too strongly when I say that a church in the land without the Spirit of God is rather a curse than a blessing. If you don't have the Spirit of God, you stand in somebody's way. You are a tree bearing no fruit, standing where a fruitful tree might grow.

I beseech you, let the Holy Spirit work through you. Give yourself as an instrument in the hands of God. Be a clean, clear channel for the Spirit to work through. This will mean control of speech, dedication of life and submission to His holy will.

Believe me: He does want to work through you!

III. HE CAN ONLY DO HIS FULL WORK WHEN WE ARE FILLED WITH THE SPIRIT

Any message on the Holy Spirit to Christians misses the mark unless we deal with this fact: "Be filled with the Spirit" (Eph. 5:18).

Fullness means emptiness of self.

Fullness means surrender.

Fullness means willingness.

Fullness means abundance.

When we have the Holy Spirit, we have all we need.

When Bishop Simpson preached years ago in Memorial Hall in London, he preached quietly but with such power that the whole assembly, as if moved by an irresistible impulse, arose at the climax of his message and, after a second or two, sank into their seats.

A professor of elocution was there. A friend, who knew that he had come to criticize, asked him after the service how he liked the bishop's elocution. "Elocution!" he exclaimed. "That man doesn't need elocution! He's got the Holy Spirit!"

That was the secret back of the attracting power of Jesus Christ. And the Holy Spirit tells the story of every great preacher whom God has used in the drawing of souls to Himself.

Yes, the fullness of the Spirit means Holy Spirit power. Listen to these plain and irresistible words: "But ye shall receive power, after that the Holy Ghost is come upon you: and ye shall be witnesses unto me both in Jerusalem, and in all Judaea, and in Samaria, and unto the uttermost part of the earth" (Acts 1:8).

There is no dearth with God. He does all things in abundance. Our part is just to let Him have His way.

Now, let us get some things clear. First, the Lord Jesus was full of the Holy Ghost. "And Jesus being full of the Holy Ghost returned from Jordan, and was led by the Spirit into the wilderness" (Luke 4:1).

On the day of Pentecost the disciples who testified in such a mighty way were filled with the Holy Spirit. "And they were all filled with the Holy Ghost, and began to speak with other tongues, as the Spirit gave them utterance" (Acts 2:4).

Peter, that mighty man of God who testified with such eloquence and power, depended wholly upon the Spirit. "Then Peter, filled with the Holy Ghost, said unto them, Ye rulers of the people, and elders of Israel" (Acts 4:8).

Again we read: "And when they had prayed, the place was shaken where they were assembled together; and they were all filled with the Holy Ghost, and they spake the word of God with boldness" (Acts 4:31).

Stephen, the man whose brief history has shaken, moved and changed the lives of so many, was full of the Holy Spirit. "But he, being full of the Holy Ghost, looked up stedfastly into heaven, and saw the glory of God, and Jesus standing on the right hand of God" (Acts 7:55).

Of Barnabas it was said, "For he was a good man, and full of the Holy Ghost and of faith: and much people was added unto the Lord" (Acts 11:24).

Of Paul we read, "Paul, filled with the Holy Ghost, set his eyes on him."

Of the disciples in Iconium we read, "And the disciples were filled with joy, and with the Holy Ghost" (Acts 13:52).

See the importance of this matter from the Word of God? God desires that His people be filled with the Holy Spirit.

I read this sentence in a book: "It is a sin for a Christian not to be filled with the Holy Spirit." I thought, *Could it be so?* Is it true that it is wrong not to be filled with the Holy Spirit? Is it a sin not to be everything God wants you to be? God grant that we might take this matter seriously.

It was D. L. Moody who said:

> I would rather be the means under God of stirring up the Christian church than winning a hundred souls to Christ. If I could stir up a hundred Christians and induce them to seek this gift of service, to get full of the Holy Ghost, it would result in thousands of conversions.
>
> When we were in Philadelphia, a woman asked me, "Mr. Moody, can women have this power?" I told her that I saw no reason why anyone should not have it who wanted to work for God. Women need it as much as men.
>
> "Well," said she, "if I can have it, I want it. I have also a Sunday school class, and they are unconverted."
>
> A week from that time she came to me and said, "I've got it! The Lord has blessed me. My husband has been converted and five of my Sunday school class."

That was the result of this woman's receiving the power of the Holy Ghost.

It spread all through the church of which she was a member, and the people, seeing that she had something which they had not, began to inquire. As a result of the quickening of that woman, five hundred members were added to the church.

28 The Christian's Memory

"And they remembered his words."—Luke 24:8.

There is an old legend about Aaron, the fisherman, who lived on the banks of a river. Walking home one evening after a hard day's toil, he was dreaming of what he would do when he became rich. Suddenly his foot struck against a leather pouch, filled with what seemed to him small stones. Absentmindedly he picked up the pouch and began throwing the pebbles into the water.

"When I am rich," he said to himself, "I'll have a large house." And he threw a stone. "And I'll have servants and rich food." He threw another.

This went on until only one stone was left. As Aaron held it in his hand, a ray of light caught it and made it sparkle. It was then he realized that it was a valuable gem and that he had been throwing away the real riches in his hand, while he dreamed idly of unreal riches in the future.

When Christians forget, they are throwing away precious blessings. Forgetfulness will rob us of the jewels which will make us rich.

We should endeavor to train our memories that they might assist us in living the happy, useful, Spirit-filled life.

Memory is trained by association: Associating one thing with another will bring to mind what we desire to remember.

Memory is trained by repetition. We should pick out what we want to remember, associate it with something or someone else, then often repeat the matter to ourselves.

We need to remember when we were saved. This should not be hard. Salvation brings joy and happiness. Psychologists tell us we remember pleasant situations more easily than unpleasant ones.

Salvation should be the greatest memory that you have. You should associate your salvation with the greatest joy you have ever known. You should rethink it, relive it.

The Apostle Paul told the church in Philippi that there were some things to be forgotten: "Forgetting those things which are behind." He did not mean the glorious experience of his salvation, for Paul remembered the day Jesus saved him and told it over and over again. He associated his meeting with Christ with the great transformation of his life.

Yes, there are some things we need to forget: many of our failures and our successes, our slights and our persecutions, harsh words spoken against us. But remember your salvation.

Some of the strongest Christians I have known have been those who have made much of the experience of regeneration. They have not hesitated to repeat telling this experience again and again. I have noticed also that to outstanding Christians, the experience maintains its newness. It does not get old with the telling.

Again, we should remember the times of special blessings. Has God answered prayer for you? Then why forget this? Associate answered prayer with the experience of praying and the sense of wonder when you saw God had done a remarkable thing for you. Allow this answer to prayer to encourage you to pray more.

Did God raise you up from a bed of illness? What a blessing to remember!

Remember also that all you have and all you are comes from Him. We are nothing in ourselves. He is everything.

When the conquering proconsuls returned to pagan Rome to celebrate their triumph, the custom was to assign each a slave whose only function was to remind the conqueror constantly that the greatest human glory passes quickly. This slave would crouch in the victorious warrior's chariot, whispering as the conqueror rode along triumphantly, "Remember! Remember thou art mortal."

One historian remarked that, because of this custom, many

swelled heads and rash, prideful deeds were averted: "Remember thou art mortal."

You need to remember daily: your weakness and His strength, your inability to cope with life's situations and His power.

As our thoughts are on remembering, as taught in the Bible, three lines of thought I would like to follow:

I. SCRIPTURAL ADMONITIONS TO REMEMBER

When Moses stood beyond the Jordan River with the people of Israel and gave the messages recorded in the book of Deuteronomy, he repeated a number of times, "Beware lest ye forget." He sought to associate the blessings of God which they were to have in Canaan land with the deliverance of the Lord from Egypt. Hear him as he said, "Then beware lest thou forget the Lord which brought thee forth out of the land of Egypt from the house of bondage."

All the way through the book, the great lawgiver called upon the people to remember—remember God's love, remember God's commandments, remember God's leadership, remember God's faithfulness.

In the book of Ecclesiastes, young people are called upon to do some remembering: "Remember now thy Creator in the days of thy youth, while the evil days come not, nor the years draw nigh, when thou shalt say, I have no pleasure in them."

The days of youth are good days, useful days, but dangerous days. Therefore, young people are called upon to remember God. Youth can be thoughtless and forgetful. The wise man said, "Remember now thy Creator."

In Luke 17:32 we have a strange admonition: "Remember Lot's wife." The context is speaking of the second coming of Christ. Jesus told His disciples that, as it was in the days of Noah and Lot, so will it be in the day of His coming. "In that day, he which shall be upon the housetop, and his stuff in the house, let him not come down to take it away: and he that is in the field, let him likewise not return back." The next verse says, "Remember Lot's wife."

It was Lot's wife who, when the angel was leading Lot and his family out of condemned Sodom, looked back upon the city and turned into a pillar of salt. She was still concerned about her house, her furniture and the affairs of Sodom.

Christ is saying that, in the day of His coming, we are to "remember Lot's wife," not to look back. We are to have no fond attachments to the things of this world but be consumed with this glorious truth: He is coming!

The Word contains many other admonitions to remember, but these samples will encourage us to study this theme and to remember those vital things which are given to us in the Bible.

II. THE WORK OF MEMORY IN THE CHRISTIAN'S LIFE

The Christian must work to keep memory alive, especially in certain matters. We may easily forget some things, but other things we are to remember.

Memory will bring into our lives blessings which we sorely need. First, consider the work of memory in prayer. Jesus said,

"Therefore if thou bring thy gift to the altar, and there rememberest that thy brother hath ought against thee; Leave there thy gift before the altar, and go thy way; first be reconciled to thy brother, and then come and offer thy gift."—Matt. 5:23, 24.

Sin hinders giving, and sin hinders prayer. The Bible says, "If I regard iniquity in my heart, the Lord will not hear me." To offer an acceptable gift to the Lord, things must be right between us and our brethren. To pray so as to get God's ear, we must get things straightened out.

If you come to pray and remember that there is something between you and a brother in Christ, Jesus says to quit praying and go make things right. If there is malice in the heart, get it out. If we need to beg for forgiveness of one we have wronged, then let's do it. If there are debts to be paid, if we have dealt unfairly with anyone, then quickly correct these things so you can pray acceptably to God.

It is my conviction that much time is wasted in prayer. I know that this sounds strange, but that time is wasted when we try to pray and we are not right with God. Isaiah 59:1,2 tells us:

"Behold, the Lord's hand is not shortened, that it cannot save; neither his ear heavy, that it cannot hear: But your iniquities have separated between you and your God, and your sins have hid his face from you, that he will not hear."

Therefore, when you come to pray, let memory work. If there is ought between you and another or between you and God, get it straightened out at once. Don't be forgetful, but remember.

Second, remember in times of slackness. "Remember how short my time is: wherefore hast thou made all men in vain?" (Ps. 89:47).

Each day we should be reminded of the brevity of life and its uncertainty. We are but a vapor that appears for a little while, then vanishes away. Redeem the time, because the days are evil.

Memory should give urgency. Remember the frailty, the uncertainty of life. Remember the nearness of death and the coming of our Saviour.

It is a dull and stupid man who drifts through every day thinking he has plenty of time—therefore, there is no need for hurry. A foolish person forgets the uncertainty of his life and wastes his days until time runs out.

Third, in times of doubt and fear, remember. When the disciples came to the tomb where Jesus had been buried, they found the stone rolled away and the body of Jesus gone. As two men in white apparel stood nearby, the disciples were afraid. These two angelic messengers asked:

"Why seek ye the living among the dead? He is not here, but is risen: remember how he spake unto you when he was yet in Galilee, Saying, The Son of man must be delivered into the hands of sinful men, and be crucified, and the third day rise again. AND THEY REMEMBERED HIS WORDS."

Jesus had taught the disciples so carefully. But their memories were so short and their minds so slow that, when He died, they didn't understand His death. When He was buried, they didn't expect Him to rise again. But then when He did rise and the angels repeated His words, they remembered His words.

Store up the sweet promises of God in your heart. There will come doubts and misunderstandings. There will come hours of gloom and despondency. It is then when you will need to remember His words. When things are happening which you cannot understand, it is good to remember that the Word says, "And we know that all things work together for good to them that love God, to them who are the called according to his purpose."

We should endeavor to store up the Word in our hearts. I was inspired by the story of the blind man in Miami, Florida, who has memorized six thousand verses of Scripture.

The more we know of this Book, the greater will be our faith. The more we hide the Word in our hearts, the purer will be our lives. David said, "Thy word have I hid in mine heart, that I might not sin against thee" (Ps. 119:11).

Fourth, remember when sin enters. When the slightest sin starts to rear its head, remember the hatred of Jesus for sin. Remember the condemnation of the Bible against sin. Remember that all sin is against God.

As Jesus was being tried, Simon Peter sat in the outer court. When a maid came along and accused him of being one of the followers of Christ, he denied and cursed. Three times this happened. Then there came the crowing of the cock. "And Peter remembered the word of the Lord, how he had said unto him, Before the cock crow, thou shalt deny me thrice." Now he went out and wept bitterly.

Simon Peter was impulsive, hasty, hardheaded; but at least he had a memory which worked; and when he found himself slipping into sin, memory reminded him of the words of Jesus. When the cock crew, he went out and wept bitterly.

Are you being tempted and tried? Then remember the words of the Scripture. There is a word to help you in every time of need. First Corinthians 10:13 has been of help to many:

"There hath no temptation taken you but such as is common to man: but God is faithful, who will not suffer you to be tempted above that ye are able; but will with the temptation also make a way to escape, that ye may be able to bear it."

O Christian, let your memory work. Let it work to make your prayers effective. Let it work to take out the slackness. Let it work to help in the hours of doubt and sin. Let memory work!

III. CONSIDER MEMORY IN ETERNITY

Paul wrote, "So then every one of us shall give account of himself to God." Memory will certainly be working at the judgment seat of Christ. God will bring to our remembrance our lives, our deeds, our works; then we must give account of them before our Saviour. "For we must all appear before the judgment seat of Christ; that every one may receive the things done in his body, according to that he hath done, whether it be good or bad."

Let the Christian remember that, if death comes, there will still come memory. All things will not be blotted out. Your works, your service must yet appear before God.

But perhaps the most fearful working of memory will be in the eternity of the lost.

In Luke 16 we have the familiar story of the rich man and Lazarus. Lazarus was a beggar who was laid at the rich man's gate full of sores. Both men died. The curtain is pulled back, and we see the beggar carried by the angels into Abraham's bosom. The curtain is pulled back for the rich man, and in Hell he lifted up his eyes, being in torments! He saw Abraham afar off and Lazarus in his bosom.

We hear the rich man cry, "Father Abraham, have mercy on me, and send Lazarus that he may dip the tip of his finger in water and cool my tongue, for I am tormented in this flame."

But Abraham said, "Son, remember that thou, in thy lifetime receivest thy good things, likewise Lazarus evil things, but now he is comforted and thou art tormented."

What a fearful phrase—"Son, remember that thou, in thy lifetime. . . ." Jesus said that in eternity, in the place called Hell, memory will live forever and ever. A man's lifetime will be remembered. He will remember his good deeds, and he will remember his bad deeds. He will remember his abundance or his poverty. Yes, he is going to remember.

Memory will be a curse in Hell. Memory will repeat again and again the opportunities to be saved—the invitations to salvation, the prayers of others, revivals, evangelistic campaigns.

Sinner friend, memory will remind you of this very service if you should die without Christ. Memory in an eternal Hell would remind you of these words I am speaking and the invitation song which we will sing in a moment.

If we will take away all of the Scriptures which teach of the fire of Hell and the torment and suffering caused by the flames, we would still have enough suffering to make the hardest sinner tremble if he would consider this matter of memory.

In closing, Christian, remember to let memory stir you up to new allegiance and new devotion to Christ.

Sinner, remember that Jesus died upon the cross for you. Remember that He said, "I am the way, the truth, and the life: no man cometh unto the Father, but by me." Remember there is just one way to Heaven—the way of the cross. If you reject it, then eternity will afford you plenty of time to remember your sinful life.

Come to Jesus now. Come for the cleansing of every sin. Make this hour a new beginning.

29 Firsthand Knowledge

"Jesus answered and said unto him, If a man love me, he will keep my words: and my Father will love him, and we will come unto him, and make our abode with him."—John 14:23.

"That I may know him, and the power of his resurrection, and the fellowship of his sufferings, being made conformable unto his death."—Phil. 3:10.

In my travels to distant parts of our nation, quite often I tell people of the beauty of Chattanooga. I mention Lookout Mountain, Signal Mountain and Missionary Ridge. I talk about the historic spots around our city. I mention the scenic railway, the Chickamauga Battlefield and other points of interest. Usually there is a dull look to the eye—no sparkle—no eager saying, "That's wonderful! I would like to see it."

There is something quite important about seeing a place firsthand. We like to see things with our own eyes. We may be pleased or displeased, but our curiosity is set at rest.

It is important to experience certain things, to know them firsthand. We can explain, describe and paint pictures, but a person must know.

The spies were sent out to view the land of Canaan and to bring back a report to the wandering Israelites. They did so, but in spite of some evidences of Canaan's fruitfulness, the people turned down the idea of going in. Caleb and Joshua felt the job could be done, but the others could not be persuaded.

The talk of the "land flowing with milk and honey" was not enough. They had not seen it. They had no firsthand knowledge.

My friends, this Bible tells us that we can know our Lord "firsthand." We are told that we can walk with Him and talk with Him. Jesus tells us in John 14 that He and the Father will make their abode with us.

Let me see if I can break this down for our thinking.

We must have firsthand knowledge

I. REGARDING SALVATION

Nothing else will suffice. Our knowledge must be experimental. It is not enough just to hear others talk about salvation; it is not enough just to read about salvation—we must know about it for ourselves.

The unbelieving critics can always give so many adverse reasons for turning from Christ. But they have never turned to Him; they do not know Christ. They simply know His name and something that might have been said about Him.

The skeptic said to a Christian worker some time ago, "I am an infidel."

"Have you ever read the Bible to seek to know if you are right or wrong?"

"No, I am an infidel."

"Have you ever read any book on Christian evidences or investigated the question?"

"No, I am an infidel."

"Have you ever by thought and prayer honestly sought to test the question?"

"No, I am an infidel."

"Why, my friend," said the Christian, "you are not an infidel."

"Yes, I am," emphatically replied the man.

"Oh, no! You are certainly not an infidel. You are a fool."

The man is foolish who tries to say that Christ, the Bible, salvation, prayer and all of these things are unreal when he has never tested them.

I must listen to my Christ. How simple and beautiful are these words, "Verily, verily, I say unto you, He that believeth on me hath everlasting life" (John 6:47).

Can you find any sweeter words than these: "Verily, verily, I say unto you, He that heareth my word, and believeth on him that sent me, hath everlasting life, and shall not come into condemnation; but is passed from death unto life" (John 5:24)?

John 9 has a beautiful story about a man who was born blind. This man was healed by the Lord Jesus. He received his sight. The Pharisees came against him and said, "Give God the praise: we know that this man is a sinner," referring to Jesus Christ. Here is the "blind" man's reply: "Whether he be a sinner or no, I know not: one thing I know, that, whereas I was blind, now I see."

Later Jesus found the man and said to him, "Dost thou believe on the Son of God?" Jesus revealed Himself to the man. We find him saying, "Lord, I believe."

This man received a firsthand knowledge of the Lord Jesus Christ.

This is exactly what the Apostle Paul had: ". . . for I know whom I have believed, and am persuaded that he is able to keep that which I have committed unto him against that day" (II Tim. 1:12).

> Amazing grace! how sweet the sound,
> That saved a wretch like me!
> I once was lost, but now am found,
> Was blind, but now I see.

That's the testimony of a man who was deep in sin, then was touched by the grace of God and brought to salvation.

The late Dr. M. R. DeHaan said:

> Salvation by faith in Jesus Christ is one of the most momentous transactions imaginable. We are made alive after being dead in trespasses and sins. The greatest evidence of the power of the Gospel is the change it produces in the believer. The thief is made honest. The harlot is made virtuous. The blasphemer is a worshiper. And the liar is dependable. The world has no answer to a changed and godly life.

Dr. DeHaan told the story of the old Fijian chief and an English earl, an infidel who visited the islands.

The Englishman said something like this to the chief: "You are a great chief, and it is a pity you have been so foolish as to listen to the missionaries who only want to get rich off you. No one nowadays believes anymore in that Book which is called the Bible. Neither do men listen to that old story about Jesus Christ. People know better now, and I am only sorry for you that you are so foolish."

When he said that, the old chief's eyes flashed, and he answered: "Do you see that great stone over there? On that stone we smashed the heads of our victims to death. Do you see that native oven over there? In that oven we roasted the human bodies for our great feasts.

"Now, you! If it had not been for these good missionaries, that old Book and the great love of Jesus Christ, which has changed us from savages into God's children—you!—you would never leave this spot. You have to thank God for the Gospel; otherwise, you would be killed and roasted in yonder oven, and we would feast on your body in no time!"

Firsthand knowledge of Christ! Thomas believed in Jesus Christ; but when he was absent on that first Sunday evening that Jesus appeared to His disciples, Thomas said, "Except I shall see in his hands the print of the nails, and put my finger into the print of the nails, and thrust my hand into his side, I will not believe" (John 20:25).

After eight days, Jesus appeared again. This time Thomas was in their midst. He told Thomas to "Reach hither thy finger, and behold my hands; and reach hither thy hand, and thrust it into my side: and be not faithless, but believing."

Thomas answered and said, "My Lord and my God."

Then Jesus said something to Thomas that I want you to notice very carefully: "Thomas, because thou hast seen me, thou hast believed: blessed are they that have not seen, and yet have believed" (John 20:29).

We can have firsthand knowledge of our Saviour as we read this infallible Book and receive Him.

I must have firsthand knowledge

II. REGARDING PRAYER

Prayer is for every Christian. Christ exhorts all to pray. The writers of the New Testament urge all to pray. Paul said, "Pray without ceasing."

It is not enough to read about Praying John Hyde, George Mueller, Robert Murray McCheyne: I myself must know that prayer is real, firsthand. I believe that these men prayed and got answers and, for that same reason, I can come with confidence before God and pray and receive answers also. Jesus says to me, as He said to men of old, "If ye shall ask any thing in my name, I will do it" (John 14:14).

The mighty power of prayer is illustrated in Jonathan Edwards. It is said that, when he preached his famous sermon, "Sinners in the Hands of an Angry God," he read from a small manuscript that he held so close to his face that no one could see his countenance. He read on and on, but the people in the crowded church were tremendously moved.

One man sprang to his feet, rushed down the aisle and cried, "Mr. Edwards, have mercy!" Others grabbed hold of the back of the pews, lest they should slip into perdition. They were under such conviction that they felt as if the day of judgment had already dawned upon them.

There was a real spiritual reason behind the power of that sermon. For three days Edwards did not eat a morsel of food nor close his eyes in sleep. Over and over again, he was heard to exclaim, "O God, give me New England! Give me New England!" When he finally got up from his knees and made his way to the pulpit, he looked as if he had been gazing straight into the face of God. Before he ever opened his lips to speak, great conviction fell upon his audience.

God wants us to pray. It is not enough to read of Abraham's prayer life, Moses' fervency, David's eloquence in prayer, Elijah's faith, Daniel's consistency in prayer. We ourselves must pray. We must know the reality of prayer firsthand!

I must know the promises that God has given me regarding prayer. I must lay hold upon the Old as well as the New Testament promises. I must believe this promise of II Chronicles 7:14, "If my people, which are called by my name, shall humble themselves, and pray, and seek my face. . . ." I must believe this just as much as I believe the promise of the Saviour when He said, "Ask, and it shall be given you; seek, and ye shall find; knock, and it shall be opened unto you" (Matt. 7:7).

Not only must I know the promises, but I must act upon them. This verse has always disturbed me: "Ye lust, and have not: ye kill, and desire to have, and cannot obtain: ye fight and war, yet ye have not, because ye ask not" (James 4:2).

I must receive God's promises and pray—pray for myself and my needs; but I must cease not to pray for others.

This week I have had a very unusual experience. I went to see a lady in the hospital. I frankly asked, "What is your trouble?"

She answered openly, without tears, "I have a cancer. It is quite serious. The doctors do not believe that I have long to live."

I said to this Christian woman, "Since you seem to have such a short time, I know you want to do something for others."

"Yes, I do," she replied.

I said, "One great thing you can do for many people is to pray for them. I would appreciate your praying for me, but pray also for your loved ones and friends. You know God answers prayer."

She said, "Yes, I know this, and I will spend more time in prayer."

I must learn firsthand

III. REGARDING CHRISTIAN GIVING

"But this I say, He which soweth sparingly shall reap also sparingly; and he which soweth bountifully shall reap also bountifully. Every man according as he purposeth in his heart, so let him give; not grudgingly, or of necessity: for God loveth a cheerful giver."—II Cor. 9:6,7.

The tithing promises of God have meant so much to me, and especially the great promise in Malachi 3:10:

"Bring ye all the tithes into the storehouse, that there may be meat in mine house, and prove me now herewith, saith the Lord of hosts, if I will not open you the windows of heaven, and pour you out a blessing, that there shall not be room enough to receive it."

It will do us good to read also Malachi 3:8, 9 and 11.

Abraham tithed. Moses tithed. The Jews tithed. The tithe is commended by the Lord in Matthew 23:23.

Thank God, I know about tithing firsthand. I know that God keeps His Word regarding the tithe. For more than forty years I have been giving a tithe of all God places in my hand—yes, much more than a tithe; and I have known the blessing of God in abundance.

You, too, must know. Take God at His Word. See it for yourself. Simply believe the promise of God's infallible Word and obey it.

When the Queen of Sheba heard of the fame of Solomon, she came to Jerusalem to see for herself that which the king possessed. She saw his riches, his fame, the house which he had built, and said, "Behold, the half was not told me."

When I speak about scriptural giving, the half has not been told. You will have to experience this for yourself, firsthand.

I must know firsthand

IV. ABOUT HIS COMPANIONSHIP

"Jesus answered and said unto him, If a man love me, he will keep my words: and my Father will love him, and we will come unto him, and make our abode with him."—John 14:23.

What beautiful words! We find the divine appreciation—". . . my Father will love him." Here is given the divine approach—". . . we will come unto him." Here is the divine abode—". . . and make our abode with him." How amazing that God dwells in our midst—yes, in us!

Enoch knew companionship with God, for the Bible says, "And Enoch walked with God. . . ."

Have you felt His presence in time of distress? Worry is so common among us. We find troubled hearts everywhere.

A picture captioned "The Face of America" appeared on the cover of one of our leading magazines. It had been taken at the intersection of two busy city streets. The people, evidently unaware of the photographer as they hurried on, revealed not one smiling face.

I made the question, "Is that the face of America? Is everybody unhappy?"

Wanting to double-check the depressing revelation of that picture, some people sent a man to the same intersection with a sack of one thousand silver dollars. He was instructed to stand there from sunup to sundown and give a dollar to any who came along looking happy, whether they were smiling or not.

At evening the man trudged away having passed out only 740 silver dollars.

This could be a picture of our time. This is a day of anxiety, not a time when men and women feel the presence of God.

Bishop Quale, an aged preacher of another century, sat up very late one night worrying. Finally he seemed to hear a voice say to him, "Quale, you have worried long enough. Go on to bed now, and I'll watch over the world the rest of the night."

Very good advice for us all, for our God "shall neither slumber nor sleep."

Have you felt His presence in the hour of sorrow? Have you heard Him say, "Let not your heart be troubled: ye believe in God, believe also in me"? God knows your trouble, your sorrow, your heartaches. And He is standing right by your side to give comfort.

Dr. T. DeWitt Talmage and his wife came home one day to find their little girl playing serenely in the living room. But as soon as the child saw her mother, she began to cry. Mother picked her up, hugged her and asked what was wrong.

"I hurt my finger."

The maid came back into the room and said in surprise, "Why, I didn't know you hurt your finger. When did you do that?"

The child admitted between sobs that it had happened some time ago.

Mother asked, "Well, why are you crying now?"

The little girl, revealing an emotion felt by the whole world, said, "I didn't have anybody to cry to before."

An ancient king brought together a great number of scholars to write a history of mankind. They compiled many thick books. Under the pressure of his duties, the king didn't have time to read them.

Finally in the sunset years of his life, he brought the same men to his palace and commissioned them to make a summary of the history for him.

One of the group spoke up: "Sir, I can do that right now in three statements: Man was born. He suffered. He died."

In a sense, the story is true, but not completely so. This is not the full story of the child of God. We have One with us in the time of sorrow. Jesus is with us when our loved ones go from us. He is with us when we come to the last mile of the way.

He is present when persecution comes. And come it will.

Daniel had persecution, but God was with him. Paul had persecution, but in the prison cell he could rejoice; for God was with him. John had persecution, but from the isle of Patmos he could shout out his song of rejoicing. We too can have firsthand knowledge about His companionship.

God is with us.

We must know firsthand

V. ABOUT COMPASSION

Jesus looked upon the multitude and had compassion for them.

Compassion is a strong word, literally meaning "suffering together with." That is precisely its meaning here as used to describe His feelings. He actually suffered in His compassion for men. His heart bled and broke for sorrowing and sinning humanity.

When Jesus saw the multitudes, He "was moved with compassion toward them" (Mark 6:34). Why was this? "...because they were as sheep not having a shepherd." This is truly a pathetic picture. Jesus cared!

It should trouble me if I don't care for others. It is necessary that I care for those lost in sin.

God will give us compassion, first, when we remember what we were. This takes us back to the time when we were lost, condemned sinners, before we came to the Lord for salvation.

Second, God will give us compassion when we see others around us lost, doomed and damned. This picture must not escape the Christian's heart. We must see our loved ones, our kinfolk, our neighbors, our friends as lost without Christ.

Third, God will give us compassion when we see what God can do. Salvation is yours, salvation is mine. Because of this, we should have compassion on others.

Kipling wrote, "The human soul is a very lonely thing. We are born alone. We die alone. And in the depths of our souls, we live alone."

Kipling was right except for one thing—salvation in Jesus Christ. When we accept the Lord Jesus Christ, He comes in to abide.

I refer you again to the blessed verse that I have used as a text: "If a man love me, he will keep my words: and my Father will love him, and we will come unto him, and make our abode with him." The Christian is not alone—Christ is with him.

If you have never accepted the Lord Jesus Christ, we bid you to come to Him now. This is the best opportunity you will ever have!

30 The Devil and Angels

"Then the devil leaveth him, and, behold, angels came and ministered unto him."—Matt. 4:11.

Three persons are mentioned in our text: Satan, angels and Christ. Satan tempted the Lord Jesus, endeavoring to make Him fail, but Jesus defeated him with the Word of God.

Satan wars against every gospel preacher, every gospel church, every gospel missionary, and every work of God. Satan warred against the Lord Jesus then, and he wars against Him now. When Jesus had finished His combat with Satan, the angels came and ministered unto Him.

Now, consider Satan, the angels and Christ.

I. SATAN

First, notice what the Word says about him. In Isaiah 14:9-15, we find the picture of Satan cast out of Heaven.

"Hell from beneath is moved for thee to meet thee at thy coming: it stirreth up the dead for thee, even all the chief ones of the earth; it hath raised up from their thrones all the kings of the nations.

"All they shall speak and say unto thee, Art thou also become weak as we? art thou become like unto us?

"Thy pomp is brought down to the grave, and the noise of thy viols: the worm is spread under thee, and the worms cover thee.

"How art thou fallen from heaven, O Lucifer, son of the morning! how art thou cut down to the ground, which didst weaken the nations!

"For thou hast said in thine heart, I will ascend into heaven, I will exalt my throne above the stars of God: I will sit also upon the mount of the congregation, in the sides of the north:

"I will ascend above the heights of the clouds; I will be like the most High.

"Yet thou shalt be brought down to hell, to the sides of the pit."

Again, the Word says that he deceived Adam and Eve. There was one tree in the midst of the garden of which God said, "Ye shall not eat of it"; but when Satan came and deceived Adam and Eve, they partook of the tree. When they did so, sin passed upon the entire human race.

Again the Bible says Satan has a lying, deceptive character:

"And the Lord God said unto the woman, What is this that thou hast done? And the woman said, The serpent beguiled me, and I did eat."—Gen. 3:13.

"But I fear, lest by any means, as the serpent beguiled Eve through his subtilty, so your minds should be corrupted from the simplicity that is in Christ."—II Cor. 11:3.

Satan's power to deceive will be felt after the thousand-year reign of Christ on the earth. We find in Revelation 20:7, 8 these words:

"And when the thousand years are expired, Satan shall be loosed out of his prison, And shall go out to deceive the nations which are in the four quarters of the earth, Gog and Magog, to gather them together to battle: the number of whom is as the sand of the sea."

We turn to II Corinthians 2:11 and find this admonitory word given by Paul:

"Lest Satan should get an advantage of us: for we are not ignorant of his devices."

The Devil works in many subtle ways to deceive both the children of God and the children of Satan.

An illustration of Satan's subtilty and slyness is in this story.

Some years ago in a certain community, parents were alarmed over the peculiar symptoms manifested by their children upon returning from a certain school. After an investigation, it was found that in front of the school an old man was wont to sell chocolates to the children. Now this old man was a decoy of certain drug merchants who furnished him with chocolates in which small doses of morphine had been mixed. The thought was that these children, who in perfect innocence had spent their money for chocolates, would be easy prey in later life and the future of these merchants of drugs would be secure and their business a going concern.

What a picture this is of the Devil! He will do anything to deceive. He will hide behind a thousand masks, play any role if only he can gain his end.

These are but a few things that the Bible has to say about Satan.

Second, the world ought to know about Satan, this deceiver of nations and of individuals.

"In whom the god of this world hath blinded the minds of them which believe not, lest the light of the glorious gospel of Christ, who is the image of God, should shine unto them."—II Cor. 4:4.

"I know thy works, and where thou dwellest, even where Satan's seat is: and thou holdest fast my name, and hast not denied my faith, even in those days wherein Antipas was my faithful martyr, who was slain among you, where Satan dwelleth."—Rev. 2:13.

"And the great dragon was cast out, that old serpent, called the Devil, and Satan, which deceiveth the whole world: he was cast out into the earth, and his angels were cast out with him."—Rev. 12:9.

Satan is a deceiver of nations and of individuals. Beware! Don't allow yourself to be hooked by Satan's many devices.

Third, you should know that Satan is the enemy of your soul, the trickster of the universe and a blockade to spiritual progress.

Christian friend, be on your toes, be constantly aware of this adversary. Do not give him one single inch. Never allow one single particle of your life to be under the sway of the evil one. Enough said about Satan.

We turn now to the second part of the message.

II. ANGELS

". . . angels came and ministered unto him."

The Bible speaks of angels 248 times. In the book of Daniel, two great angels are mentioned—Michael and Gabriel. In Daniel 12:1 we have mention of Michael:

"And at that time shall Michael stand up, the great prince which standeth for the children of thy people: and there shall be a time of trouble, such as never was since there was a nation even to that same time: and at that time thy people shall be delivered, every one that shall be found written in the book."

Michael's name is also given in Jude 9:

"Yet Michael the archangel, when contending with the devil he disputed about the body of Moses, durst not bring against him a railing accusation, but said, The Lord rebuke thee."

In Daniel 8:16 we have mention of Gabriel:

"And I heard a man's voice between the banks of Ulai, which called, and said, Gabriel, make this man to understand the vision."

Gabriel is God's messenger. It was Gabriel who came to Zacharias and told of the birth of John the Baptist:

"And the angel answering said unto him, I am Gabriel, that stand in the presence of God; and am sent to speak unto thee, and to shew thee these glad tidings."—Luke 1:19.

Gabriel came also to Mary and gave the message to her of the birth of Jesus (Luke 1:26-38).

Second, angels were present in the ministry of Jesus. They ministered to Him after His temptation in the wilderness (Matt. 4:11). The angels came down to strengthen Jesus after His tempting in the garden of Gethsemane: "And there appeared an angel unto him from heaven, strengthening him" (Luke 22:43).

An angel gave the message of the resurrection of Jesus to the women who came to the tomb (Matt. 28:2-7).

There were three royal witnesses of the resurrection of Jesus. The first angelic witness is described here in Matthew 28. The other two are given in John 20:11 and 12:

"But Mary stood without at the sepulchre weeping: and as she wept,

she stooped down, and looked into the sepulchre, And seeth two angels in white sitting, the one at the head, and the other at the feet, where the body of Jesus had lain."

Third, angels helped the saints of God, pictured for us so beautifully in Acts 12:7-9. Peter was in prison. The angel came and told him to gird himself and bind on his sandals and to follow him. Peter did so and was delivered from the prison.

Angels come to encourage us in the time of distress:

"For there stood by me this night the angel of God, whose I am, and whom I serve, Saying, Fear not, Paul; thou must be brought before Caesar: and, lo, God hath given thee all them that sail with thee."— Acts 27:23, 24.

Can't you see that angels are given to help and encourage us in times of difficulty?

Fourth, angels watch over our children. "Take heed that ye despise not one of these little ones; for I say unto you, That in heaven their angels do always behold the face of my Father which is in heaven" (Matt. 18:10).

This reading comes out of what may be called the children's chapter of the Bible. The child is mentioned seven times. The disciples were arguing about who would be the greatest in the kingdom. Jesus and His disciples were perhaps in the home of Peter, a married man. Jesus, no doubt, took one of Peter's children and gave His disciples a very pointed object lesson. He informed the disciples that small children are recognized in Heaven—"In heaven their angels do always behold the face of my Father which is in heaven." Jesus is telling us that children have guardian angels watching over them. This is a thought worthy of contemplation.

Fifth, angels are coming with Christ when He returns:

"For the Son of man shall come in the glory of his Father with his angels; and then he shall reward every man according to his works."—Matt. 16:27.

"When the Son of man shall come in his glory, and all the holy angels with him, then shall he sit upon the throne of his glory."—Matt. 25:31.

"And to you who are troubled rest with us, when the Lord Jesus shall be revealed from heaven with his mighty angels,

"In flaming fire taking vengeance on them that know not God, and that obey not the gospel of our Lord Jesus Christ:

"Who shall be punished with everlasting destruction from the presence of the Lord, and from the glory of his power;

"When he shall come to be glorified in his saints, and to be admired in all them that believe (because our testimony among you was believed) in that day."—II Thess. 1:7-10.

These verses are enough to show the great place angels have in the ministry of spiritual things. They work with our Saviour, they worked with the Apostle Paul, and the angels of God have a place in future events.

III. CHRIST

"The devil leaveth him, and, behold, angels came and ministered unto him."

The place of safety is close to His side.

When Christ walked upon this earth, He was victorious when Satan tried to tempt Him. Satan seemed to have succeeded when Christ died; but Christ was victorious, and the Devil was defeated. Our Lord arose from the dead.

Christ was the enemy of Satan. So must we be.

Where is our safety? In Christ.

First, receive Jesus Christ as your Saviour. There is no safety until He is your Saviour. Without Christ you are condemned, without God and without hope. You are weak and easily deceived; but with Christ as your Saviour, you are saved forever and secure in Him.

Second, not only receive Christ as Saviour, but rest in Him and find peace, comfort and delight in His presence. Christ can give us what we so desperately need.

Phillips Brooks once said:

> Here is a man who was born in a lowly manger, the child of a peasant woman.
> He grew up in an obscure village.

He worked in a carpenter's shop until He was thirty; then for three years He was an itinerant preacher.

He never wrote a book. He never held an office. He never went to college.

He never owned a house. He never had a family. He never traveled two hundred miles from the place where He was born.

He never did one of the things that usually accompanies greatness.

He had no credentials but Himself.

He had nothing to do with this world except the power of His divine manhood.

While still a young man, the tide of popular opinion turned against Him. His friends ran away. One of them denied Him.

He was turned over to His enemies. He went through the mockery of a trial.

He was nailed upon a cross between two thieves.

His executioners gambled for the only piece of property He had on earth while He was dying—His coat.

When He was dead, He was taken down and laid in a borrowed tomb through the pity of a friend.

Nineteen wide centuries have come and gone.

Today He is the centerpiece of the human race, and the leader of the column of progress.

I am within the mark when I say that all the armies that ever marched, all the navies that were ever built, all the parliaments that ever sat, and all the kings that ever reigned put together have not affected the life of man upon this earth as powerfully as has that One solitary life.

Jesus Christ *was* the Son of God. He *is* the Son of God! He gives everlasting life unto men who believe in Him.

He invites you to come to Him and to obtain everlasting life through His name. Come to Jesus! Come with all of your fretting, cares and worries. Come to the Saviour with every weight and burden pressing upon you.

The most precious of all verses in which Jesus said "Come" is found in the book of Matthew: "Come unto me, all ye that labour and are heavy laden, and I will give you rest."

Come was Jesus' word to His disciples, calling them away from their former activities to Him and a new life.

Come was His word to John and James, to Peter and Andrew,

calling them away from their boats and nets to become fishers of men.

Come was His word to Matthew (Levi), sitting at the seat of customs.

Come was His word to Zacchaeus the publican, to the rich young ruler, to every one of the twelve disciples, and to the seventy.

Yes, it is the word of Jesus to you today—"Come unto me!" Come to Jesus and obtain everlasting life.

31 Christ in the Center

"Then the same day at evening, being the first day of the week, when the doors were shut where the disciples were assembled for fear of the Jews, came Jesus and stood in the midst, and saith unto them, Peace be unto you."—John 20:19.

Men are ever seeking for success in life. They spend themselves, their talents, their time, endeavoring to reach the place of success.

There are some who want to be successful in the field of money, yet how little money can purchase! Money cannot give us peace nor joy. Money cannot give opportunities for spiritual service. Money cannot bring man into the family of God.

Someone has written it down like this:

> In decimal money, a billion is a thousand million. If you had a billion single dollar bills and desired to count them, it would require over thirty-one years to do so, counting at the rate of one a second, twenty-four hours a day. If a generous billionaire wished to give away ten thousand dollars every day, he would have to live more than two hundred seventy-three years to accomplish it.

It is hard to understand the field of money as expressed in this day. We talk about putting seventy billions of dollars into this program or that program. Our nation is so many billions of dollars in debt. But when all is said and done, all the money in the world cannot purchase salvation nor give to us peace and joy.

Still others seek success in fame. Fame soon fades away. The famous of yesterday are forgotten today.

Others seek success in position. They want elevation in life, the high place. But this, too, quickly vanishes. The high place is often taken by another, and we are relegated to a secondary position.

What success can we have in life? The only guaranteed success is to make Christ the center. When Christ is all and in all, when He fully controls your heart and life, then your life is successful.

This success you can have now. It is not necessary for years to go by. It can be otained in youth, in old age, in middle age, in illness, in good health. You can have this success which is above all others the moment you determine He shall occupy the central place in your life.

Christ must be the center of all things. Now, let us study this for a moment.

I. INTERNATIONAL AFFAIRS FAIL WHEN CHRIST IS NOT IN THE CENTER

The world was never in a more precarious condition than now. This is a time of atom bombs, H-bombs, nuclear bombs and satellites. This is a time of hatred between nations. The world is uncertain.

Is there an answer? Yes. The only answer is Christ in the center. But this is too sound, too fundamental, too elementary for the great nations of this world. They want to shut Christ outside. Some disregard Him, some hate Him—only a few want to follow Him. But the only answer to our international crisis is Christ in the center.

II. CHRIST IS THE CENTER IN BUSINESS

What a difference it would make if Christ were recognized as standing in the center of every business! Shady deals would be on the outside. Doubtful methods would be discarded.

What is the need in business? For business to be operated on the "God-standard." We will continue to have strife and bloodshed in the industrial world until Christ becomes all and in all. He must be the center in business.

III. CHRIST MUST BE IN THE CENTER IN SOCIAL LIFE

What place does Jesus have in the dancing, the parties, the drinking, the drugs, the unrestrained flesh of present-day social life?

Christ can give nothing but a stinging rebuke to those who go on in the delirium of this present world.

But all of this does not change the fact that He still needs to be the center of social life. Social life should be, and can be, built around Him.

IV. CHRIST IN THE CENTER IN HOME LIFE

What does it mean for Christ to be in the center of your home life? That your home will have a family altar, that there will be a definite time each day when the Bible is read and prayer is offered. Shame upon the Christian home that does not have a family altar!

Christ in the center will mean that Christ will direct the members of the family to the house of God. Church attendance is of primary importance. There is no way for this matter to be overemphasized. It is impossible to place too much stress upon attendance at the house of God. Your home will fail unless every member in it is faithful in church attendance.

It is appalling how many mothers and fathers turn their children loose and do not require them to attend church. Mothers, fathers, you will pay the price for this tragic and awful sin—a sin against your children and a sin against yourselves.

Again, Christ in the home will mean right living. Right living excludes drinking, drugs, profanity, pornography, and evil speaking. If Christ is in your home, then you will live right and be separated from the world. What marvelous changes will take place when Christ is in your home!

V. CHRIST IN THE CENTER IN CHURCH LIFE

It is sad to say, but in many churches the Lord Jesus is not in evidence. The sermon does not point to Him. The activities of the church do not revolve around the Saviour. The message of redeeming grace is not given to the people.

Many churches are rich, but poor in spiritual living. Many are rich, but poor in sound teaching. They follow the lines of modernism. Many churches are rich, but have low standards.

Quite often Christ is not in the center of the lives of the leaders of the church.

A young man of my acquaintance is having great spiritual difficulties. This has led him away from the Lord to drinking and perhaps to other sins. He has been saved, or so he testified.

He went to see a minister about his troubles. After a few moments in the preacher's study, the minister opened a box of cigars and offered the young man a smoke. Although he smoked, he would not smoke there and said, "No, thank you."

The preacher took a cigar, lighted it, talked with him a few moments, then told this young man he believed everything would turn out all right. And without a word of prayer or any concrete advice, he sent him on his way.

Beloved, Christ must be in the center of our churches. He must control every avenue and channel of our work. He must be in our Sunday school, our training union, our preaching services, our prayer meetings—the Lord Jesus must be first. He must have central place!

VI. CHRIST IN THE CENTER IN YOUR LIFE

All must begin with you! All else fails unless He has the place of preeminence. Whether your pathway is successful or depressing, whether you are in sickness or in health, whether in happy times or sad times, Christ must be in the center.

Christ in the center will mean peace. Look again at our text. Jesus came inside the closed doors, stood in the midst of His disciples and said, "Peace be unto you." In every circumstance, it is the same. Christ in the center, in the midst, means peace.

Is your life troubled? Then bring Christ into the center, and there will be peace. Are you facing some serious difficulties? Let Jesus come into the center and watch every difficulty fade away.

A man went one night to hear a sermon on consecration. No special message came to him until the speaker knelt to pray. As he did so, he uttered this sentence, "O Lord, Thou knowest we can trust the Man who died for us."

The friend said God spoke to his heart, and he knew that was the message he needed. He went out of the building with this sentence ringing in his heart: "You can trust the Man who died for you." This statement brought him face to face with himself. He yielded his whole life to the Lord—every talent, every energy—then he stated, "I will trust the Lord to lead me. Since He died for me, surely He can give me the guidance I need."

Christ in the center will mean peace and purpose to your life. Are you wondering what to do next? Then rest it all in His hands. Let Him direct you and give you the purpose.

As I thought of this message, my mind went to the story of H. G. Spafford. He had been a very successful lawyer in Chicago; then there came a serious financial crisis, and he lost it all.

In order to get his wife and children away from Chicago and the time of readjustment that he was facing, he decided to send them to visit friends in Europe.

They left on a French liner. In mid-ocean the steamship collided with another; and in twelve minutes the French ship had gone down, carrying to death 230 souls, among them the four daughters of Mr. Spafford. Mrs. Spafford sank with the vessel, but floated again and was finally rescued.

Those rescued were taken to France; and from there Mrs. Spafford sent a message to her husband in Chicago: SAVED, BUT ALONE. WHAT SHALL I DO?

This message of fearful import, sufficient to drive reason from its throne, was the first notice Mr. Spafford had of the disaster. What had happened to his dear ones since he parted with them a few days before in New York?

When he reflected that his property was lost, his wife was painfully prostrated, his four children were buried in the dark waves of the sea, there came from his heart a song of resignation and of trust— a song which has been sung many times around this world.

> When peace like a river attendeth my way,
> When sorrow like sea billows roll;
> Whate'er be my lot, Thou hast taught me to say,
> It is well, it is well with my soul.

Mr. Spafford went to Europe, got his wife, brought her back to this country and said, "I never felt more like trusting God than I do now." He went through his days fully trusting in the Lord and making Christ the center of his life.

 **Stir Thyself**

"And they were the more fierce, saying, He stirreth up the people, teaching throughout all Jewry, beginning from Galilee to this place."— Luke 23:5.

"Now while Paul waited for them at Athens, his spirit was stirred in him, when he saw the city wholly given to idolatry."— Acts 17:16.

"Wherefore I put thee in remembrance that thou stir up the gift of God, which is in thee by the putting on of my hands."—II Tim. 1:6.

"Yea, I think it meet, as long as I am in this tabernacle, to stir you up by putting you in remembrance."—II Pet. 1:13.

"This second epistle, beloved, I now write unto you; in both which I stir up your pure minds by way of remembrance."—II Pet. 3:1.

The words of His enemies as given in Luke 23:5 are an indication of the effectiveness of the Saviour's work among the Jewish people. They said of Him, "He stirreth up the people." How did He stir them? By His teaching!

Oh, that our Saviour might walk into our midst and stir us up!

Some of you might envision the mighty words of Christ and their effect upon our society. But I have news for you: we have His words now. This Bible has for us the words of our Saviour! What we need is holy men to declare His Word!

We need also holy ears to hear His Word. Jesus said, "He that hath ears to hear, let him hear." A physical deafness is overtaking us.

In conversation with a medical man some days ago, he commented on the poor hearing of some people today. Then he went on to talk about the loud, raucous sounds of this hour—public address systems, radios, television sets, a constant pouring of sounds into our ears. I think he is right! We hear less and less, and pay less and less attention to what we do hear.

But if this is happening in the physical, how much more in the spiritual! Men are hardening themselves against all spiritual understanding. So many Bibles in the homes, so many religious broadcasts on radio have causes many to harden their hearts against things spiritual.

May we be stirred to a new zeal—a new compassion—a new understanding.

I. STIRRED BY SIN

Sometimes we look around us and wonder if anything stirs people in this day of sin, wickedness, lewdness, hypocrisy, this day of plenty and prosperity, this day of the abundance of many things.

Not only is this a day of wickedness, but this is a day of tragedies. We see them, hear about them on every hand. This is the day of sorrow and bloodshed.

Strangely, preachers are not stirred by sin as they once were. I hear more and more about ministers who are giving up their convictions about strong drink, smoking, immorality and other sins of the world. The very things that one day drew the heaviest denunciations from the ministers of the Gospel, today are excused and even engaged in by many who profess to be the spiritual leaders.

Churches do not stand against sin as in the early days of this dispensation and in the early days of our nation.

Parents do not declare themselves against evil as once they did. There is a sore tendency to compromise. Perhaps the reason many parents do not speak out against sin is that they engage in it themselves.

First, be stirred by the sins that drag men down. Don't allow Satan to deceive you. Don't be ignorant of his devices. See the results of drunkenness, immorality and dope.

Second, be stirred by the sins that break and destroy homes. Every day we read of a large number of divorces, divorces even in our city. What are the sins that are breaking homes? I could mention many of them, but the sin that I preach against so often is the sin of unfaithfulness to the house of God.

Third, be stirred by the sin that damns the souls of men, the sin of unbelief. Jesus said, "He that believeth on him is not condemned: but he that believeth not is condemned already, because he hath not believed in the name of the only begotten Son of God" (John 3:18).

The sin of unbelief is the sin of all sins. It is the only sin that damns. Here is the sin that damns and gives nothing in return.

The sin of theft usually gives some satisfaction in getting something without paying for it. The sin of lying may have a compensation in deceiving somebody. The sin of gambling has its pay in getting something for nothing. The sin of drink has refund in the feeling and the effect of satisfying the thirst. The sin of the lust of the flesh pays off in the gratification of fleshly desires. **But the sin of unbelief has no reward, no recompense, no pay.**

Here is the wicked sin that damns the eternal soul of man! Do not allow yourself to think of this sin as being negligible. This is the sin of all sins. All sin is against God, but this sin condemns the soul into Hell forever.

Be stirred by the awfulness of sin!

II. STIRRED BY SOULS

We come now to speak of the need of the eternal soul. It is this that should stir us. Christ is our example. He shows us how our hearts should be stirred to compassion for the souls of men. "But when he saw the multitudes, he was moved with compassion on them, because they fainted, and were scattered abroad, as sheep having no shepherd."

In the Gospel of Mark, the word *compassion* occurs again and again. "And Jesus moved with compassion." And again, "And Jesus, when he came out, saw much people, and was moved with compassion toward them...."

Here we must exercise great care. This is a selfish, self-centered world. It is not concerned about others; and unless we exercise great care, we will allow ourselves to be turned away from a compassion for souls. Our compassion must reach out to those around us. Our compassion must extend to the ends of the earth. We must ever concern ourselves for missions. If we fail to be missionary minded, we fail to stand in the place of divine blessing.

Men need Jesus Christ! Men need salvation!

Dr. Arthur Fox got to thinking so much about this so great salvation that he put together a number of thoughts that are superb. Listen to some of them:

> Salvation is great because of its conception and its cost. It was conceived back in the secret councils of God in His infinite wisdom, love and mercy. No man could have thought out such a way of salvation. It is above him, it is beyond him, it is of superhuman intelligence.
>
> But think what it cost God to work out this way of salvation. The Bible tells us that He gave His only begotten Son. Jesus came and died for sinners. God Himself ordained that this is the way of salvation. Jesus came to die that sinners might be saved.
>
> Salvation is great because of its extent and its eternity. The Bible says, "Whosoever will may come." This means all classes of humanity from any part of the earth, anybody and everybody who will come to Jesus Christ. The deepest dyed sinner may have the happiest hope of a heavenly home if he will only come.
>
> This is the extent of salvation, but we remind ourselves that salvation is eternal. For the Bible says, "He that believeth hath eternal life."
>
> Salvation is great because of its freeness and fullness. This salvation is a free gift. "For by grace are ye saved through faith; and that not of yourselves: it is the gift of God: Not of works, lest any man should boast" (Eph. 2:8,9). You cannot buy it, beg it, borrow it, nor steal it. You cannot merit it nor inherit it. Salvation is the gift of God. It is free, but it is also full. When a man accepts this salvation, he has something that lasts forever. It is completed and cannot be depleted nor repeated.
>
> Salvation is great because of its pardon and its peace. The Word says, "Let the wicked forsake his way, and the unrighteous man his thoughts: and let him return unto the Lord, and he will have mercy upon him; and to our God, for he will abundantly pardon."
>
> God rejoices to pardon the penitent sinner; but in our salvation we also have peace. Peace is calmness of soul—it is the soul's

right relationship with God. When we come to the Lord Jesus Christ, we have peace with God.

When we do God's will, we have the peace of God.

This salvation is great because of its way and its warning. There is a simple way and solemn warning. How simple and beautiful is salvation! A poor sinner can come. The weakest individual can be saved. The most illiterate can repent and believe.

How great is this salvation because of its simplicity!

But there is also a warning. Salvation gives a warning. There is one way of salvation, and that is in Jesus Christ the Saviour. Therefore, men must believe in Jesus Christ if they are to be saved.

God grant that we might be stirred by the need of lost souls, stirred so much that we will give ourselves to witness to them. God can use any one of us to win souls if we will but do His bidding.

III. STIRRED BY THE SAVIOUR

First, we talked about being stirred by the sin which surrounds us; second, we are stirred by the condition of lost souls; third, we are stirred by the Saviour.

Look upon the One who died for you upon Calvary's cross. Look upon Him who was buried in the tomb and arose the third day. Look upon Him who ascended on high and is now at God's right hand interceding for us.

Contemplate the greatness of the Son of God. Meditate on the purpose of His coming into the world.

When Pilate questioned Jesus, "Art thou a king then?" Jesus answered, "Thou sayest that I am a king. To this end was I born, and for this cause came I into the world, that I should bear witness unto the truth. Every one that is of the truth heareth my voice" (John 18:37).

A newspaper article was recently carried by the *Chattanooga Post.* The big headline read, "New Look at Old Issue: JEWISH LEADERS SOUGHT TO SAVE JESUS, JUDGE SAYS."

The first paragraph of the article reads, " 'Ancient Jewish officials sought to save Jesus from Roman execution, but He wouldn't cooperate,' says a noted authority on first-century Jewish and Roman law."

The article has to do with the "findings" of Justice Haim Cohn of Israel's Supreme Court. His findings were recently published and hence the write-up in the paper.

He says that the Sanhedrin endeavored to save the life of Jesus, but He would not cooperate. He states that the Sanhedrin did not want to kill Jesus because the popularity of the high priest of the high court had been diminishing among the people. Hence, if they could have saved Jesus, it would have raised the people's estimation of the court.

Justice Cohn says that it was for this purpose, after the Sanhedrin had discredited the witnesses, that its president, the high priest, questioned Jesus directly, asking if He was "Christ, the Son of the blessed." Jesus replied affirmatively. That reply "caused the high priest and the Sanhedrin to give up in despair," the judge said.

Since Jesus would not "bow to their authority" or give the assurances that they needed to intervene in His behalf, the judge said, "They could do nothing more." In other words, they could not do anything else but let Jesus be tried and condemned.

But, my friends, think for a moment. What else could Jesus say? He *was* the Son of God. He could not tell a lie. He said, "I am the way, the truth, and the life." When the high priest questioned Him, "Are you Christ, the Son of the Blessed?" He had to say yes, for that He was.

You see, there is something that the world misses: Jesus came into the world to die. Listen to these words of our Saviour:

"Therefore doth my Father love me, because I lay down my life, that I might take it again. No man taketh it from me, but I lay it down of myself. I have power to lay it down, and I have power to take it again. This commandment have I received of my Father."—John 10:17,18.

The judge also tries to say the Jews did not crucify Jesus. Jesus was crucified by sinners—Jew and Gentile. The sins of the world rolled on Him. He died for us. In I Corinthians 15:3 the Apostle Paul expresses it in this way: "For I delivered unto you first of all that which I also received, how that Christ died for our sins according to the scriptures."

I would have you to be stirred by a suffering Saviour—stirred by the Christ who died upon the cross for you.

Paul ever looked to the Lord Jesus. When he went to the city of Athens and saw the idolatry, the Bible says, "His spirit was stirred in him." It troubled him that they were worshiping idols made with hands.

We, too, need to be troubled, for everything that competes with God is an idol. It may be a loved one whom we love more than God. It may be self. It may be business or a cherished ambition or career. If it crowds God out or gives Him second place, it is an idol.

Don't be passive regarding this matter, but be deeply stirred by the idolatry of our modern civilization. In reading Acts 17, you will see that Paul was not stirred because of the murders and the riots in the city, but he was stirred by their idolatry! This should stir us. We should be incensed by anything that comes between us and our Saviour.

Paul hated idolatry. He sought to bring the minds of people to see the Christ. Paul had a hatred for all religious forms. Of himself he said:

"If any other man thinketh that he hath whereof he might trust in the flesh, I more: Circumcised the eighth day, of the stock of Israel, of the tribe of Benjamin, an Hebrew of the Hebrews; as touching the law, a Pharisee; Concerning zeal, persecuting the church; touching the righteousness which is in the law, blameless."—Phil. 3:4-6.

Paul had a hatred for an empty religion—a religion that does not give peace or power.

Does your heart go out to the masses who have nothing? Our city is filled with those who have only empty religions. I want to be kindly toward the various types of religious organizations of this day, but I must be honest. All religions fail that do not center in Jesus Christ.

The religion of good works is empty.

The religion of baptismal regeneration is empty.

The religion of church membership is empty.

The religion of sincerity is empty.

There is but one true religion—one faith—that is, faith in Jesus Christ. He is the Saviour. Jesus said, "I give unto them eternal life; and they shall never perish."

33   Living Faith

"And Jesus answering saith unto them, Have faith in God."—Mark 11:22.

We are commanded by the Lord Jesus, "Have faith in God." Disobedience to the Lord's command is a serious sin.

The exhortation to have faith in God is one of the most important words given by our Saviour, the one thing most disregarded by Christians. Most people pray but exercise little faith in God. They pray but do not expect anything to happen. Many live separated lives but do not have faith in God. Many study the Word but do not have faith in God. Multitudes engage in Christian service but fail to exercise faith in the Heavenly Father.

"Have faith in God" is one of the most important statements given by our Lord.

Now observe the following:

First, living faith is tied to a Person—to Jesus Christ who never fails. A living faith is not tied to a book nor to a motto or some slogan, but tied to a Person. Look to Christ and believe in Him.

Second, living faith is tied to a principle. What is that principle? That God is honest, that God will fulfill every word which He has spoken. If you read a promise in this Book, then have faith in God to know that He will fulfill and do what He has promised to do.

Third, living faith is tied to a practice. In the past, our God did not fail. In the present, faith in Him has been sufficient for every need. And we can rest on His Word that in the future He will never forsake His own nor turn away from their repeated cry.

With this as an introduction, I give four statements regarding living faith.

Living faith is a

I. SURPRISING FAITH

When the Christian begins to exercise faith in God, he is surprised at his own peace of heart, surprised at the rest given him through faith.

Living faith will surprise you! Let the troubled soul receive this Word. Rest fully and completely upon the promises of God. If your faith is at first weak, then keep building upon it until it is strong and worthwhile.

Second, not only will your faith surprise you, but your faith will surprise others. Have the kind of faith in God that will cause people to be amazed. It is true that at times people may laugh at you because of your faith. They may feel that you are foolish to have great faith. Again, some may wonder at your faith. They may be puzzled by it and wonder how it could be. But, best of all, some will desire your great faith in God. And this is the happy part: faith is available for all men.

George Mueller had faith in God. His faith was so great that he built an orphanage and operated it for about sixty years without asking anyone for help. He took his burdens to the Lord, and God answered prayer. The entire world has been surprised at the faith of this great man.

But along with our surprise, we have received encouragement because we know that the God who answered his prayers can answer ours also.

Third, living faith will please God. This is the very thing that God wants you to have. He wants you to have peace of heart because of your faith in Him. In Hebrews 11:6, the great chapter on faith, we find these words, "But without faith it is impossible to please him: for he that cometh to God must believe that he is, and that he is a rewarder of them that diligently seek him."

Is it in your heart to please God? Surely you want to do that which will please the Father. Then, my friend, have faith in God.

Living faith is a

II. STIRRING FAITH

No one can have faith in God without being stirred to activity and obedience to the Lord. Faith will stir us to work. When faith is small, work will be small. If you are doing little for Jesus, then it is an evidence that you have a small faith, for great faith in God will seek expression and will find it in active work.

The Bible tells us about Andrew's coming to Jesus. After he came to the Saviour, he went out and found his brother Simon Peter and brought him to Jesus. He said, "We have found the Messias, which is, being interpreted, the Christ.... And he brought him to Jesus."

What was Andrew doing? Exercising himself in service because of his faith in Christ. His faith was a living faith that stirred him to action.

Let me give another illustration.

Saul of Tarsus sought in every way to destroy the Christian faith, but on the road to Damascus he was struck down by a light from Heaven. The Lord spoke to him, and Saul was convicted and converted. He became a man of God and perhaps the world's greatest preacher.

Paul had faith in Christ. What did this faith do? It set him to preaching, teaching and winning souls. Notice in Acts 9:20, "And straightway he preached Christ in the synagogues, that he is the Son of God."

Paul wasted no time. He got busy at once. His faith demanded expression, and he gave expression by launching out in work.

Inactivity of Christians is an indication of their lack of faith. They are not stirred to activity because they have only a small faith in God.

Allow me to suggest three things that a stirring faith will do:

First, a stirring faith will make us rejoice in what we have. We will rejoice that we are saved and on the road to Heaven. We will rejoice that our names are written down in the Lamb's Book of Life.

Second, a stirring faith will make us see the need of others. We will be like the four men who brought the palsied man to Jesus. They had a faith that stirred them to believe that Jesus could help their palsied friend; therefore, they brought him into Capernaum and to the top of a house. They uncovered the roof and let down the sick man before Christ.

The Bible tells us, "When Jesus saw their faith, he said unto the sick of the palsy, Son, thy sins be forgiven thee." It was a stirring faith that caused them to bring the sick man to Jesus. Jesus saw their faith and healed the sick.

Third, stirring faith makes us rejoice in His ability to do all things. Stirring faith will continue to make us see that God is not limited. He can do the impossible.

Living faith is a

III. STABILIZING FAITH

We have touched on two points of this message: living faith is a surprising faith, and living faith is a stirring faith. Now, let us see that living faith is a stabilizing faith.

Who is the steadiest person you know? You answer: "The man with faith in God." It has ever been so, that a man with faith in God is steadfast.

Living faith will make us steadfast in times of storm. By storms I mean the heartaches of life, the tragedies, the difficulties, the sorrows.

Some months ago I preached in the Mel Trotter Mission in Grand Rapids, Michigan. One day I went down to the basement of the building to the barber shop to get my shoes shined. I sat down in a chair, and an old black man began to shine my shoes.

After awhile I asked, "Have you been at this job very long?"

"Yes, I have had the job for fifty-one years."

"But how old are you?"

"I am eighty-one years of age."

Then I asked him, "Are you a Christian?"

Big tears came to the old black man's eyes as he answered, "Yes, sir, I have been saved for many years. I am a deacon in the church. I witness daily to sinners. I know that Jesus is my Saviour."

As I kept on talking to him, he told me that he was from

Greeneville, Tennessee. "I am the last of a big family. All of my children are dead. I buried their bodies in Greeneville, Tennessee." But he said, "I am still victorious! One day I'm going to see my loved ones again. It won't be long because I'm getting old."

As he told me the story, there was a smile on his face and big tears from his eyes.

Yes, faith will keep you steady in times of storm. Since we know not what may come on tomorrow, we can only say, "Have faith in God."

Eight days ago four girls in this city had a mother and father. A week ago tonight mother and father were suddenly killed. What a storm for young people! How much they need faith in God!

Mr. and Mrs. Frank Qualls of Brownsville, Texas, were visiting the Grand Canyon with their two children. They stopped the car, and Mr. and Mrs. Qualls got out to look at the giant gorge. Suddenly they saw their car move. In a moment's time it had plunged fifteen hundred feet down in the Grand Canyon. James Lloyd, five years old, and Harold Frank, fifteen months old, died in the plunge.

What could sustain mother and father after such a tragedy? Only a living faith in Christ Jesus. Miserable, unhappy, and all of their days will be spent under a cloud without faith. But if they know Christ, they will know that one day there is coming a joyous reunion.

Second, living faith will make us steady in the time of illness. These bodies are weak. Sickness lays hold upon us. So we must have a strong faith to keep us going on.

But when people fail to have this faith, what happens? Their lives are due some tragic thing which brings sorrow down upon many others.

Many years ago I held a meeting in Cookeville, Tennessee. After one service, one of the young ladies of the choir went home and killed herself. Mother and father had been in the service of the church, and the daughter went home ahead of them. When they arrived, she was dying. She failed to have faith to keep her steady in the time of illness.

On June 9, 1958, bloodhounds found the body of Donna Reinhold, eighteen years of age, hanging from a tree in a wooded area. The girl had killed herself. Her mother said that she had been physically ill for some time and had stated that she would be "better off dead."

What can sustain young people? Living faith in a living Christ. What can sustain mothers and fathers? Living faith in a living Christ.

Living faith is a

IV. SAVING FAITH

What is a lost man's chief need? Christ—to touch our Saviour, to come in contact with the One who saves, keeps and satisfies.

On last evening I had the joy of leading two young men to Christ. One young man came up on the platform after the service. He towered above me some three or four inches. He shoved two dollars in my hand and said, "I want to give this to you."

I quickly asked him, "Are you a Christian?"

"No," he said.

"You need to be," I replied.

He said, "I know I do."

I gave him the Word of God and prayed with him, and there on the platform he entered into the family of God and became a child of God through his living faith.

Sinner friend, trust Christ as Saviour. Know that He will do for you that which needs to be done.

Christian friend, exercise faith in God. Be strong because of your living faith in a living Saviour.

For a complete list of books available from the Sword of the Lord, write to Sword of the Lord Publishers, P. O. Box 1099, Murfreesboro, Tennessee 37133.